Baptized Rage, Transformed Grief

Baptized Rage, Transformed Grief

I Got Through, So Can You!

CHERYL A. KIRK-DUGGAN

Foreword by Traci D. Blackmon

RESOURCE *Publications* • Eugene, Oregon

BAPTIZED RAGE, TRANSFORMED GRIEF
I Got Through, So Can You!

Copyright © 2017 Cheryl A. Kirk-Duggan. All rights reserved. Except for brief quotations in critical publications or reviews, no part of this book may be reproduced in any manner without prior written permission from the publisher. Write: Permissions, Wipf and Stock Publishers, 199 W. 8th Ave., Suite 3, Eugene, OR 97401.

Resource Publications
An Imprint of Wipf and Stock Publishers
199 W. 8th Ave., Suite 3
Eugene, OR 97401

www.wipfandstock.com

PAPERBACK ISBN: 978-1-5326-3613-4
HARDCOVER ISBN: 978-1-5326-3615-8
EBOOK ISBN: 978-1-5326-3614-1

Manufactured in the U.S.A. 11/13/17

In Honor and Memory:
Hon. Michael Allan Kirk-Duggan

God-fearing, Family man, Devoted Husband, Genius, Sage,
Humorist, Marvelous Friend
who has always believed in the good and the best,
who gifted with empathy, listened and loved well

Contents

Foreword by Traci D. Blackmon | xi
Acknowledgements | xiii
Introduction | xv

Deserts, Wells, Stalactites | 1
Now, Before, Then/Later | 2
Whirling Rivers | 4
Soaring | 5
No Baptism, No Tears | 6
Waters of the Deep | 7
Torrential Rains | 9
If I cry | 10
Dripping Anger | 11
Baptized Rage | 13
Angry Cells, Skewed Waters | 14
"Mists of Fury": Predatory Unfurled | 15
Angered Sweat | 16
Fiery Puddles | 17
Bitter Tears | 18
Disappointed Streams | 19
Addictive Waters | 20
Ragged Rain | 21
Damned Spot | 22
Agitated Monsoons | 23
Ragged Dewdrops | 24
The Strain | 25
The Heavy Feet | 27
Missed Thoughts | 28
Overwhelm | 29

Clouds Dancing | 30
Steaming Rage | 31
Pissed Ire | 32
Tormented Downpour | 33
Dripping Pain (Anguish, Angst | 35
Putrid Fog | 36
Engorged Pools | 37
Tearful Hurt | 38
Thunderous Insanity | 39
Ruptured Fluids | 40
Liquid Agony | 42
Baptized Rage: Grief Reconciled | 44
Volcanic Rain | 46
Used, Abused, Discarded | 47
The Grief Cycle | 48
Angry Waters | 50
Musings before Noon | 52
Numbed Silence | 54
Stunned Grief | 56
Wet Grief | 58
Cruel Madness | 59
Fainting Mists | 60
Bastardly Betrayal | 62
Death: Just a Breath Away | 64
Revolutionary Revelation | 65
Mental Aerobics | 67
Starved for Rest | 68
Exposed Canvases | 69
Despairing Hues of Night | 70
Weighted by Fatigue | 72
Fatigue Revisited toward Love | 73
Speaking, Listening, Loving, Living | 75
Questions, Interrogations | 77
Yoga Moments | 79
Problems Hovering | 81
Acid Boiling | 82
Sweet Dreams | 84

Many Days before Christmas | 85
Ancient Fissures Run Deep | 88
For Mothers Who Desire | 91
Fear Visits | 94
Opportunity | 96
And Tears | 98
Sister, No Friend | 99
Uncertainty | 101
Sadness | 102
Pensive Moments | 103
Exuberant Resignation | 105
Illusive Answers | 106
Restlessness | 107
Anguished Indignation | 108
Visions | 109
Tumultuous Joy | 110
All Desire for God | 111
At Rest | 112
Seasons | 114
Joy Takes Delight | 116
Complexity of Breathing | 118
Disappointment | 119
Whispered prayers | 121
Waiting | 122
Exercises in Serenity | 123
Full Moons | 125
Fires Among us | 126
A Celebrated Life | 127
Goodnight Sun | 128
Divine Seduction | 129
An Incredible Light | 130
Mystical Moments of Joy | 131
Right with God | 132
Riding the Seas | 134
Slapped Back to Faith | 135
Another Day | 137
Restless Gratitude, Formidable Challenges | 138

Listen to Me | 139
Gift of Grief and Shame | 141
Poignant Dissonance | 142
Mysterious Moments | 144
Sad Puddles | 146
A Closed Chapter | 147
Moments, Motions, Experiences | 148
Grace & Laughter | 150
Monster Toys | 151
Fires Engulfed, Flowing Fresh Waters Heal | 153
Rage by Noon | 155
Baptized Rage Unfurled | 156
A Belly of Faith | 157
Dawn Breaks | 158
Surprises Dance in Splendor | 159
Guilty Grief | 160
Holy Bliss: A Kiss of God | 161
Crashed and Burned | 162
A Holiday from Acceptance | 163
From the Brink of a Breaking Point: This Too, will Pass | 165
An Obituary for the Never born | 167
Fleeting Furies | 168
Galvanized Grief, Gangrenous Guilt | 170
Revelation, Release, Regroup, Restore | 172
Wisp of Frustrated Reality | 173
A Volcanic Moment | 174
Vulnerability | 175
Busted | 176
Serenity | 177
Circumstances | 179
A Hot Summer's Day | 180
Trust | 182
On a Collision Course with Myself | 184
Sweet Surrender | 186
Postscript 1: Stunned Grief | 188
Post script 2: Baptized Rage, Smoldering Grief | 190
Post Script 3: Bon Voyage | 191

Foreword

THIS COLLECTION OF STORY and poetry has become my constant companion during these last few months, reminding me that our expressions of grief are in indeed as sacred as our expressions of joy. I did not realize how much I needed permission to give voice to the full range of my human emotions in times of great distress.

Rev. Dr. Cheryl Kirk-Duggan provides a roadmap to restoration by inviting us to a deeper journey with her through the inevitable disappointments of life. By sharing with us glimpses of her darker moments of despair, with transparency and grace, she reveals to us the crevices of her heart and invites us to baptism.

Dr. Kirk-Duggan invites us to a holy immersion into the depths of rage and lament that might easily consume us. She does through these writings what few dare, inviting us to the depths of the holy to hear her cries of lament and discover our own. The privilege of this literary journey continues to transform my understanding of my personal rage, our communal grief, and our God. For this, I am deeply grateful.

Rev. Traci D. Blackmon
Executive Minister of Justice & Witness
The United Church of Christ

Acknowledgements

A LIFE UNFOLDING IS a gift and blessing supreme. To chart one's experiences like a colorful tapestry woven of intricate stitches is to know a creative journey of visits to the valleys that lead us to shadows and deaths of various kinds, along with many sojourns to numerous mountaintops. Sometimes the journey is fraught with wonder, mystery, and holy surprise. Other times we have a feeling of déjà vu, like we have been there before, and we ponder questions of why, why now, and what is God trying to teach me. Sometimes reality unfolds as if this was to be. Much of what we experience, however, often seems unexplainable. We can find no logical or reasonable answers. We rehearse the story many times in our minds; sometimes we share it over and over again with friends, with no more clarity when we tell the story for the fifteenth time, than when we told it the first. Between the highs and the lows reside the day-to-day, mundane tasks of showing up, and taking care of routine business, of going to work, whether we feel like it or not, the basics of laundry, meals, doctor's appointments, church, family gatherings, and shopping.

Like you, I have lived through many such tasks on a daily basis as I have lived through the deaths of parents, friends, parishioners, cousins, aunts, and uncles.

I became caregiver, when my beloved went from decent health to a myriad of major health challenges including surgeries. Initially, he worried how I would survive six months, a year after he died. Given our incredible relationship and many in-depth conversations about life and death, he knew I would be OK. Disappointments and the trauma of grief, sadness, loss, and accompanying anger and rage often unfold amid various life experiences and changes. There are also mountain top experiences, when we find tools of empowerment and transformation, —and we are changed..... And then, one day, he slipped away.

Many have walked with me on this decade plus long journey, to whom I am grateful. I am deeply grateful to persons who created and introduced the Body for Life (exercise and wholeness) program to me: Bill Phillips,

Jerry Braam, Porter Freeman; Cindy Homan; Bambi Laird-Opeliner, the staff and students at the Berkeley Bikram Yoga studio, Berkeley, CA; and Monica Bradfield, Tiffany Ingersoll, and the other staff and students at Open Door Yoga studio, Raleigh, NC. To my colleagues from the Womanist Approaches to Religion, the American Academy of Religion, and those on the list-serv under the auspices of emilie townes and Renita Weems, and Katie G. Cannon who have encouraged me in life and in my writing tasks, thank you. My prayer buddies and cheerleaders include the late Jessie Katherine Wilson, my 83 year-old going on 38 year-old sister/mother friend, Louise Noel Williams; Sister and Brother friends, Gloria Roach Thomas, Lennie Corey, Marsha Foster Boyd, Salima Ira Swain, Stacey Floyd-Thomas, Kelly Brown Douglas, Allison Brewster Franzetti, Janice Lee, Deborah Shaw Boatner, Vanessa Wilson, Markesha Grayson; Estelle Brooks, Arnita Henson, Frank and Maelois Wilson, Adrian Fowler, Rona Drummer, Odette Lockwood-Stewart, Sharon Thornton, Karen J. Torjeson, Karen Lebacqz, the late Diane Thomas, Jane Austin, Alice Kirk Blackburn, Michelle Gonzalez, Sharon Thornton, Faye M. Morris, Opal McCoy, Bea Morris, Patricia-Ann Johnson, Evelyn Parker, Barbara Essex, Ann Jefferson, Lelia Llwelyn, Debra Mumford, Lilipiena Darensburg, Chanequa Walker-Barnes; Beverly Wallace, Evelyn Parker, Michael Hardin, Liz Alexander, Teresa Fry Brown, Ann Harris; my Sankofa elders crew: J. Alfred Smith, Sr., Addie Lorraine Walker, Rose Marden, Dwight Hopkins, Steve Reid, Thelma Chenault; Diana Hayes, Raymond Bryant, Scott Woodward, the late James Noel, and my co-laborers in the Gospel at Young Missionary Temple: Pastor Ronald L. White, Sr., LaTanya Sanders, Glenda Johnson, Angela Black, Delwyn King, Freddie McAllister, Juanita White, Ida Dawson, Leroy White, Ann and Johnny Cooper, Yvonne Mills, Leonard Cross, Cheryl Garris, Georgette Watson; and faithful friend Lannie Willie. Daughters Siobhan Smith, Cheryl Hartman, Mary Cathrine Dorney, Michelle Williams, and Michelle Craig, and sons Christopher, Robert, and Michael Duggan inspire and encourage me: my kids and their spouses and their children are so proud of their "Mom" and Grandma[1]. My sister, Dedurie Kirk, reads me so well, has always had the wisdom of a 90 year old, even when she was in elementary school, which she so generously shares with me. To the many sages who have crossed my path, many unnamed and many more recent, I am grateful to Norma Campbell, Steven Baum, Alex Elliston, Catherine Lee, Kirk Bingaman, Kim Smith, Janet Nielson, Uma Ratnam, Linda Berry, Amy Schaible, Ellen Condelli, and countless others. For the generosity of spirit and the willingness to share the moments of joy and of anguish, the Bay Area Alzheimer's Support Group,

---

1. My beautiful inherited family, where there is no distance.

Acknowledgements

Berkeley, CA, I give my thanks and prayers. To many encouraging voices I encountered during the time when grappling with critical issues I give thanks: Jean Corey, Emerson Powery, Hugh Page, and Stephanie Crowder. The support and questions of my colleagues from the Racial Ethnic Faculty Association of the Graduate Theological Union (1997–2004) was invaluable, including Fumitaka Matsuoka, Tim Tseng, Edmund Yee, George Cummings, Russell Yee, Warren Lee, Byoung Lee, and Rigoberto Calca-Rivas. To many colleagues some who began as my students, co-learners, and support staff, from whom I've learned so much, I tip my hat: Rebecca Parker, Maureen Maloney, Kathleen Kook, Arthur Holder, Robert Russell, Mary Ann Tolbert, James Donahue, JoAnne Henry, Cecelia Gonzales, Joseph de Leon; Ray Carr, Kevin Kocezula, Mary Lowe, Gerard Reid, Dan Peters, Whitney Bauman, Kimberly Whitney, Darnise Martin, Nancy Pineda, Ken Rowe, Joellynn Monahan, Michelle A. Gonzales, and Julie Stoneberg.

To my colleagues and students at Shaw University and Shaw University Divinity School, who have welcomed my prophetic voice crying in the wilderness, I say thanks: Interim President Paulette Dillard; Gaddis Faulcon, Dorothy Cowser Yancy, Tashni-Ann Dubroy, Marilyn Sutton-Haywood; Divinity School Dean Johnny Hill, Asst. Dean Jamie Ashmore, former Deans Bruce Grady and David Forbes, Sr., faculty and staff, notably colleagues Mike Broadway, Linda Bryan, Pat Powell, Mena Lewis, Stella Goldston, Reginald High, Lonieta Cornwall, Lafayette Maxwell, Brad Hunnicutt, Bobby Sanders, and Timothy Brock; of special thanks, Lizette Tapp, Tom Clark, Librarians.

And always for his love, strength, laughter, challenges, expertise, support, and comfort, I give eternal thanks to my beloved husband Mike; may he rest in peace. For years he served as chief cook, bottle-washer, cheerleader, and editor; the joy of my life. As we walked together over three decades, especially during the recent past, he showed an indefatigable relationship with God, a profound deep love and caring for me, incredible sense of aplomb, gratitude for the little things I did as caregiver, an unfathomable passion and compassion for others, an amazing sense of acceptance, and a gift for living in the moment. This work is a testament and testimony of faith, pain, joy, hurt, grace and divine mercy unspeakable.

Introduction

SOMETIMES, WE THINK WE have it all together. Others might have the same impression of us. With spouses or partners, educational degrees, a home, cars, name recognition in some circles, and modest notoriety in our chosen fields, it might appear that life is good and success abounds. And in many ways we do have, and have had it together. Yet, sometimes there are loose threads to the garment of our lives; threads that we find in the lives of others and in culture in these United States and the world. In my own life, though I was sometimes not consciously aware of it, the loose threads of anger, grief, and the related loss as betrayal were unraveling. When I was physically active, I was always more connected and at peace. Those little threads did not seem to bother me as much.

Time and time again, however, I would often get out of the habit of physical exercise. When I got too busy with work to work out, I did not have the spiritual revelations that happened when I jogged, power walked, did yoga, or circuit training. In the midst of hit and miss exercise, I could recount problems that were taking an emotional drain on me. Infertility compounded by the seeming onset of spousal Alzheimer's, seemed to push me over the edge. All hope of having children – biological or adopted, and the possibility of celebrating a 50th wedding anniversary with my beloved spouse, disappeared over the course of twenty-four months; the saga of the Alzheimer's presentation lasted roughly another four years. The threads began to disentangle. My anger seemed to be right below the surface, at the same time quite deep. Without consistent workouts, some of my senses were dulled and I was oblivious to the depths of pain. After doing yoga and later Body for Life fitness program, I really began to see the rage I could no longer deny. With all hope of having children – biological or adopted snuffed out and with my spouse seeming to lose his former genius status wit, brilliance, and cognitive ability, I became more uptight and troubled. In hindsight, I lived at the intersection of rage and grief for months. The catalyst for my initial realization and the awakening of "the Furies" began while jogging on the shores of the Atlantic, on the Island of Puerto Rico, in the shadows of Viesquez, where the United States' frequent rehearsal of bombs bursting in air was making a population deadly ill. For months I lived at the intersection of mania and misery.

I met my rage through baptism, during my dawn exercise ritual, as I rounded the curves on the track, on a beautiful, sunlit morning. The Spirit compelled me to re-experience my baptism. "You are holding on to rage about the middle passage (the experience of millions of enslaved persons packed like sardines in the bowels of ships from Africa to the Americas), and you still mourn and hurt around your parents' deaths. You have much anger regarding the death of your fetus." After our brief love affair with what we hoped would be our first born nine months later, that dream died in the time it took God to create the world, in seven days. I knew positively that I was pregnant seven days, before I had to then submit to a D & C, because there was no heartbeat.

As I continued running around the track, the voice continued, "You are ravaged by fury that must be released. You are carrying around pain that's not your own. Let it go! Rebaptize yourself in these waters, so that you can release this agony, and can be reborn and restored." I heard all of this in amazement, panting as I ran to complete one more lap, with the waves from the Atlantic lapping against the shore and the breezes rustling in the palm trees a few feet away.

Re-experience my baptism? Yeah, right. I'd heard of people doing this, but for my money, wasn't once enough? Yet, relentlessly, the Spirit tugged at my heart and kept intruding my mind. Being obedient I said, "Sure, why not?" Totally embarrassed, I told a couple of male ordained friends, for no other women clergy were present at this intense focus session of the Faith and Order Commission, National Council of Churches. I gingerly explained to them what had happened and invited their assistance. You never saw men who are usually quite suave, professional, and in control get so agitated and uncomfortable. You could see them thinking about dogma and correct practice. They were worried about protocol; I was focused on my sanity and the recent revelation. In exasperation, one said he was leaving early the same afternoon, so thank you, but no thank you. My other friend, with whom I had a much longer standing collegial relationship, made a noncommittal response and didn't bring the subject up again, even when I glanced his way knowingly. Not to be outdone, I told him of my plans for baptism the next morning before our meeting ended that night.

Morning came and he was not in the decrepit exercise room where he'd been the last two mornings. I realized for whatever reason, he was incapable of assisting me in this venture. I also realized that I could rebaptize my own self, in the spirit of the priesthood of all believers, and the gift of my own ordination. With a little trepidation, I left the hotel lobby with towels in hand, out to the beach of nearest proximity. To my relief, part of the ocean was enclosed with a reef, so I would not feel the full impact of the ocean as I began my ritual. I knew that people did outdoor baptisms in rivers or lakes, but I had neither; I had an ocean. Another part of my skittishness was not about the ritual I was called to experience, but that I am not a good swimmer. I feel safe in three feet of water, for despite my goal to enter a mini-triathlon, which requires biking, running, and swimming, the swimming and to a lesser extent, the biking is still a dream. Not to be out done, I persevered.

I sat on the concrete embankment for a while meditating on the ebb and flow of the water. I took off my running shoes and dangled my feet in the water so I could adjust to the temperature. Slowly, I waded out into the water. As I stood there, the first revelation was that what had seemed to be solid, the ocean floor, actually shifted. Every time the tide came in and went out, the sand where I'd been standing shifted, so I was slowly sinking. Each time I shifted my position on what initially felt like sturdy ground, I would feel the shifting sand beneath me, again and again. I waded further out into the water. Bravely, I lowered my body and got on my knees and let the water kiss my torso. I finally sat down on the ocean floor as the water pushed my body back and forth. When it was time for me to baptize myself, rather than push my head backwards, which is what would have happened had I had assistance, I lowered my head forward and baptized myself in the name of the Creator, in the name of Jesus the Christ, and in the name of the Holy Spirit. My mission was now accomplished; accomplished but not completed.

I heard no music, felt no overwhelming sense of peace or anxiety, and experienced nothing other than the water. Where was the chorus of angels, or the fireworks, or at least my own rapid heartbeats? Nothing happened. A little disappointed; no, a lot disappointed, I dried off, got rid of some of the sand, and then went back inside the hotel, up the stairwell, and to my room. Still nothing, though I had been obedient. Faintly resigned, I turned the shower on, adjusted the temperature and stepped in. And then, in those moments, came the release, the release that I had desired.

My tears gushed forth; my whole body shook. With the tears came a powerful spiritual, emotional, and physical release. With the release, came the second revelation. I needed to write about my rage, the anger that was brewing, fermenting beneath my skin. These boiling elements were actually, physically getting under my skin in a way that caused chronic dermatological problems, which had not been solved or even had a diagnosis that made sense. This same concretized stress was probably contributing to my weight gain; was causing me heightened tension that could make me really sick if I failed to release the fury. (Years later, the dermatological problems morphed into skin cancer (CTCL: Cutaneous T-Cell Lymphoma, Stage 1.)

So thousands of miles from home, I began this phase of my pilgrimage, May, 2001, of naming, processing, releasing, and coming to heightened sense of consciousness about the powers and principalities, and the demons, that unbeknownst to my waking self, were unraveling my serenity. I began to focus on the first line of the Twenty-Third Psalm, stressing a different word each time I said it through: THE Lord is my shepherd, I shall not want; The LORD is my shepherd, I shall not want; The Lord IS my shepherd, I shall not want, and so forth. I repeated over and over the words of the serenity prayer daily. Sometimes, all I could do was moan: an intense, resonant wailing sound would rumble from the deepest core of my being. Other times I called prayer partners, dear spiritual friends who prayed with me, who let me weep and talk incessantly. Sometimes I would meditate. Sometimes I worked out, did power walking and jogging. One gift of this journey was the efforts of my poetic muse that "came on line," and allowed for a great outpouring of anger, grief, betrayal, and loss.

Sometimes the words would flow while I was journaling. Sometimes it happened when I was on the stationary bike at the YMCA, or right after a session on the tread mill or during aerobics. After beginning Bikram Yoga, the practice that involves 26 Hatha Yoga positions twice through for ninety minutes in a room heated at 100+ degrees, I could no longer deny the feelings that would emerge. During these intense meditative postures, the issues that bubbled within me would surface. My body was no longer willing to hold on to such turmoil. Waves of nausea or tears or feelings of deep sadness announced my inner reality of emotional turbulence: feelings and realities tucked away and denied, so that I could move through life, and help others. I had been aware of some of this, but much of this melody of angst had been an unsung song in muted silence. I needed to face the facts that some days I didn't have it all together, and clearly there were parts of my life over which I had no control. Who was I kidding? I know that most days I am totally powerless over people, places, and things. On some plane, I had known this a while back, and, paradoxically, in acknowledging my powerlessness, I actually gained tremendous freedom and power. This lesson had been tucked away, however, so I wasn't experiencing a lot of freedom or sense of empowerment. I was torn, worn, and tired. I began to keep a legal yellow note pad with me for the purposes of transcribing the words that exploded within my mind, body, and spirit. Other times, I'd grab the back of an envelope. Over the course of a few years, about seventy poems on rage and grief were born. When I felt this volume culminating, over a decade had passed, and there were over 150 poems. My issues with my parents' death and infertility were the initial catalysts for some of the poems. These poems helped birth the themes that ruminate throughout this meditations.

There were mornings when I realized that I was angry at several things – too many to name. The realization exhausted me. Those were times when the only thing I could do would be to tell God all of my troubles; the God who promised in Deuteronomy 4 to never, ever forsake me. Since sometimes these revelations happened really early in the mornings, I waited until a descent hour to find a conscious, human ear to listen; to be with me in my misery. The earlier thoughts, revelations, and subsequent confession were so important. Sometimes I would pray and cry out to God, and sometimes because I was so restless, I didn't pause to listen for God's response. Sometimes I did remember that prayer is a dialogue and not a monologue, and it would be so comforting to sense God's presence and hear God's response.

Some mornings, I would wake up and it would be so beautiful, that I would get dressed quickly. I walked and ran the hills as I purged the grotesqueness of this thing, this anger and grief that literally, figuratively, and actually weighed on me and weighted me down. This thing, this angst and sorrow, this ire and woe, this rage and heartache made me feel ancient. During some moments, it would cause an incapacitating affect that thwarted my passion, the fires of joy, hope, and love.

Over time, I realized that I was so angry at God and Mother and Dad, that God let them die, and that they died. One of the reasons I felt such a deep loss, in part was that we were in the process of trying to adopt a child or children. I became so aware of their needs and that if we were blessed with little ones, they would not have any grandparents. The absence of that generation in our lives really heightened my awareness around the loss I felt with my parents' absence, and how critical grandparents are to nurturing children, and loving them well. In life, it is amazing how we reach out for others. In reaching out for someone else's children, they would become ours. Sometimes in the process I wondered if in reaching out to someone else's children, were we asking for more heartache? Our children would never ever know their grandparents on my side of the family, or my husband's[1] side. All are dead. And yes, they live within our hearts and we have pictures, and I know they are all praying for us; otherwise, we could have not been kept safe as long. I know they are in me and I in them, but they are still dead. I know Daddy's body was tired; he had fought so nobly for so long, but he still is not here. I was angry; he died only six months after Mike and I got married. He and my husband would have been such good friends.

---

1. Though writing most of these poems while Mike was alive, my best friend, lover, and spiritual companion, he transitioned this life October 1, 2011.

Clearly, I am so grateful for having him through adulthood, but I missed him so. I felt sad. I had friends, longtime friends, who were blessed to still have both parents alive. I have other friends who have one parent alive. And of course, I have other friends who for all intents and purposes are orphans. We may have a few aunts and uncles around (of my maternal uncle and aunt, and thirteen paternal aunts and uncles, only one uncle survives), but our parents, those who birthed and raised us are dead. I don't envy anyone else their wonderful blessings of parents; I grieved the loss of my own.

I still have no clue as to why God let Mother die at the young age of 62. She had so many hopes and dreams. Mother had never been sick; I can't remember her ever having a cold. The doctor diagnosed her with leukemia in May and she died in October, 1989. She had looked forward to retirement; she believed, as did we all, for her healing. She could have come to visit or live with us, and had so many new and wonderful experiences. Our friends would have embraced Mother. She never got to hold our kids; and of course, now there are no kids for her to hold. Oh the sadness and loss around this one was, is so incredibly deep. There was so much she did not get to do. There are many things I can now not share with her.

I don't deny she had a wonderful life, but the ending pain was so huge. She had lost so much by the end. She didn't smoke or drink. She was a faithful and wonderful Mother and a friend. She prayed for us, and like Dad, she loved us. Her death makes no sense to me. I know the one constant in life is that if you are born, you will die; but her death was so sudden. There are times when I feel such a loss that I cannot call her up and tell her to plan to visit. She didn't get to hold my nephew for long, or sing to him, or tell him stories about other members of our family. Seems selfish? I don't think so —- it hurts, such a deep loss. Mother, Dad, did you give up? Did your bodies give up? Did God call you and you knew not to fight anymore?

I am angry with God and with Grannie that she had Alzheimer's. What a waste, waste, waste. My beloved Grannie disappeared, and this woman left in the shell of her body was listless, fitful, no sense of humor. They tell me she could cuss like a sailor. I am deeply grateful I never witnessed any of these episodes. The contrast in the before and after is a nightmare in hysterics. She was a neat, clean, proud, yet humble woman. She loved people at church. She loved to take care of the flowers and made some of the communion linens for church. She spent hours at the church. For years, her home was the sanctuary for ministers of Reeves Temple. They knew they could find quiet and a meal at Bec's house. Thursdays at Grannie's were such an experience in collaboration and learning to pull one's weight. Among maternal extended family, we learned to set the table, and sit and eat with cousins, and how to clear a table, and how to restore a room to a previous order. One neat rite of passage was that when you began high school you could then sit at the "big table." At the big table, you got to serve yourself, listen to grown folks conversation, and participate as well. I miss that Grannie. She died in her 97th year, having had Alzheimer's for about ten years or so. The grace is that she lived long enough to see her grandchildren grown, and she shared lots of years with us, loving us, teaching us, and guiding us. She loved a lot of people and was held in high esteem by many. The beauty is that I see much of her personality in some of the grandchildren. Her legacy lives on. The legacies of all people live on, in certain traditions, when one calls out their name and remembers them. What a blessing to remember the good and beautiful amongst the pain. Sometimes we do well moving day to day; other times we are stymied and get bogged down in our realities and how we interact in the world.

One morning on the way to work I saw a deer; it had frozen in the middle of the street, and I waited patiently for it to pass. Getting anxious or blowing the horn would have only made the deer more nervous and it probably would not have moved as quickly. The sound of the horn may have traumatized the deer. Sometimes we are like deer. Sometimes we freeze when the bright lights of crisis, change, and difficulty pierce our reality. Sometimes, like deer, we eventually do move on; at other times, we get stuck in the quick sand of difficult challenges, and we remain there, especially if we do not have a community of accountability around us, to help us come back to a more balanced view of life.

During this period, I also wrote about my anger at society for viewing educational institutions, especially the soft sciences as peripheral. People entrusted with nursery schools, day care, kindergarten, and elementary schools have to purchase their own supplies and remain underpaid. There could be no successful careers and businesses without strong foundations, but those who help to provide those foundations are devalued and compensated poorly. I also realized my anger at folks who create programs but fail to work out a substantial funding apparatus across the years. The rule of thumb is that you need three to five years of capital when beginning any venture, because it will take that long before you can turn a profit. Unfortunately, many visionaries have poor business sense; consequently, many of those who work in the nonprofit sector work too hard and are often grossly underpaid. In faith communities and in higher education, there are so many incompetent people that have advanced amid the Peter Principle. They have been elevated to the height of their incompetence. Seems some of the hardest working, most talented people get the most hassles, and those that worm their way into positions ride on the coattails of those who really care and work really hard.

During that season, my daily prayer was to become aware of my emotional issues and to be able to continue to see where my anger exists. I began to reflect more on anger, research it, and took an anger management training course. One of my prayers was to be able to release more anger, and to be able to use my anger creatively. I had come to recognize that anger, like any other emotion, is not good or bad, it just is. I also recognized that sometimes when anger does exist, one may or may not be aware of it, for it may be buried underneath great hurt, grief, and loss. As I peeled back the onion of my life, I began to see that there was a place where anger and grief, betrayal and loss were intimately connected.

Who knows why there are certain issues in our lives that are hard to release? When we first got married, with school and familial financial obligations, it seemed the wrong time to think about children. Later, when we did try, our attempts seemed futile. I had lots of support dealing with our inability to conceive. Then we gave up; we realized that we would not have the blessings of giving birth to children. Then an astonishing thing happened: September, 1994, we were pregnant; unbelievable! As this was the time before everyone had home computers and internet access, we phoned and faxed everyone our great news. We were so thrilled, so delighted.

After being almost stupefied when getting the positive news from the nurse, after so many negative home pregnancy tests, I managed to ask, so now what do we do? She said to come in for a sonogram the following Wednesday, and she would give us the probable due date and get me set up with a healthy regimen. We made it to Wednesday and through morning sickness. I just knew we were having twins, as the Spirit had let me see them previously. I dreamed about them, so I'd talk to the fetuses and bargain, "Just let me get through teaching this morning and then I promise to take a nap." I would get so sleepy around mid-day, that I could fall asleep where I was sitting. Several times I woke up and then realized I had fallen asleep at my desk. I also had pulled out fabric and three patterns for maternity outfits that I'd bought several years earlier as New Year's presents for myself. The day arrived and we went to the sonogram appointment with eager anticipation. The doctor began the ultrasound exam, and then the ceiling caved in.

The OB/GYN on call (my doctor was off teaching at the VA hospital across the street) asked me if I had all of my female organs. I began to get a little nervous, but said, "Sure, I had that test already and all of my organs are doing fine." Well when a doctor, when anyone asks you if everything is in place, you know something is not right, as my husband held my hand on one side, and the nurse massaged my shoulder on the other. Then the doctor said, "Well, maybe you are earlier than we thought. By seven weeks, we should sense a heartbeat, long before we can even spot the fetus." No heartbeat; Oh, God. Then he uttered veiled words of limited assurance. "You may not be seven weeks; so, come back Friday, and if we still can't get a heartbeat, then you will have to have a D&C. We will have to get the dead tissue out of you."

Somehow, despite this ominous news, we got out of the Duke Medical complex and made it home; holding on to each other, feeling terrible. Back to hospital on Friday, we got the grim report: no heartbeat. I would soon no longer experience morning sickness. We would need to get an appointment for a Monday morning D&C. The procedure was uneventful, and by God's Grace, there were no complications. At one point, we tried a round of Pergonal, a fertility drug to boost the production of eggs. But, because I ovulated too soon we could not get everything in sync for a conception, so we decided that we would just go aux natural. Besides, fertility drugs were still relatively new, and who knew what the long term side effects might be? Years passed and we got on with our lives. After moving to California, we tried one more time.

After a television news segment on the value of acupuncture for helping some infertile women get pregnant, we tried that too. Acupuncture was great for my ragweed allergy, but was unsuccessful in treating my infertility. Then we visited an infertility clinic. On our initial visit, the fertility specialist did an abdominal ultra sound and discerned that my uterine lining was too thin to sustain a pregnancy. She then suggested that we do a series of estrogen injections to thicken the wall. If this route was successful, we would have to have donor eggs. No credible obstetrician/gynecologist would try in vitro insemination with my old eggs. This ended up being a moot point, for with two rounds of estrogen, my uterine wall remained the same. My doctor's parting words to us was that "your best option is adoption." Down but not out, we decided to adopt.

We were not looking for a genius child or Euro-American girl or boy (we were an interracial couple). We wanted a child; in fact, we said we would take a hard to place child, a child of mixed blood – actually children –an infant and older sibling. We signed up with an agency recommended by a friend of a friend, attended all the trainings, did the two home visits, got recommendations from our friends, our individual sessions, CPR and First Aid training, and had our finger prints sent off for an FBI clearance check. We were in a program called foster-adopt, where we would get the children initially as foster children and then later be able to adopt them. We went through all of this and began to think through how we would need to make our home child proof – questions of wires lying out in the open behind stereo equipment, outlets that would need safety covers, and safety locks for cabinets that prying little hands could open easily. My husband even went to extra sessions, a couple of "adoption picnics" where perspective parents could meet and visit with children who were available for foster-adoption programs. We also read a lot about adoption; and I learned that I had friends who had been adopted. So, we were set to foster-adopt, to help us get the children earlier. For seven months, we showed up, we prayed, we learned, we waited. I had even picked up a couple of little toys, because we thought that Christmas of 1999 might find the pitter patter of little feet in our hall ways.

In January, we learned that after stringing us along, the agency said they would not give us a child. They were the wrong agency for us. Seven months earlier, I thought I would have been crushed when we got the verdict that a pregnancy of any kind was impossible. I was definitely upset, but after we went full out for adoption only to be turned down again, I was devastated. This was really hard; cruel, deeply painful; unfathomable betrayal. The excuses they gave us were lousy and safe, but did not ring true. They did not seem credible, particularly when we were given no options. They told us I was too busy and that we were fixated on an infant. We had no more energy, no more fight left to try to go through this process again. Our biggest error in this process was that we did not realize that in many settings, adoption is adversarial.

When we were rejected by the adoption agency, we grieved. ""I cried again. I felt so awfully wounded and distraught. I was in deep pain and grief. I was so hurt; I could hardly be there for my husband's pain and grief. I also went through moments of incredulity. I had been prayed for and anointed to give birth. I received prophetic words from various faithful folk. In my spiritual imagination, repeating here, I had even seen the twins crawling away from me in the upstairs hallway. All to no avail. A few years later, the pain was so deep and my despondency so great, that seeing pregnant women or families with several children would literally give me an anxiety attack. Sometimes, I would sob uncontrollably. Other times when traveling in airports, I would manage to get out my cell phone and call a prayer partner to gain the strength and get connected enough to not embarrass myself. I could see how over the last few years I had been in environments, the academy, or the church, where people invariably would discuss their children and grandchildren. When reflecting, I found that sometimes my anger was present beneath the pain, sorrow, and tears. Over time, I came to realize that there was something else going on emotionally: there was a deep sense of betrayal by God and by the adoption agency. I came to see that the other side of my "baptized rage," my sacred anger, is "transformed grief."

I could see that most of the time, I was in a better place about children. When a favorite relative asked if we had had any children, I responded easily saying, we gave it our best shot. Not all of God's promises come to all of us, in life. Sometimes, I would say that I didn't give birth to babies, I birthed books. Just as it seemed that we were on an upturn, and that I was in a much better place, we got the diagnosis that my beloved probably had Alzheimer's. This agony went beyond the furthest distance in our galaxy – there are no words to indicate the level of devastation and pain. One thing my beloved most prized was his mind, with a 180+ IQ, and while he accepted the diagnosis, as a "what is, is" I was traumatized.

The first six months after we got this probable diagnosis, I was in a dazed stupor; a kind of post-traumatic stress disorder. I would say the words that affirmed his disease, but the whole experience was so surreal. My rage resurfaced fully the day we attended our first support group meeting; care givers and significant others were in one room with a therapist, and those with the diagnosis were in another room with their therapist. On that occasion, everyone in the caregivers' room, other than me was already retired. At the end of the session, everyone in the room with the diagnosis seemed to be so old—ancient, slightly disembodied, exhausted, and ever so weary. I freaked out. In that moment, I could barely breathe. What was happening to us? What was going on? I returned to my office, racked in pain, and crying torrents, as I wrote a poem, spilling out the putrid angst using language I had never thought or spoken, "Bastardly Betrayal."

The good news is that ever since his initial diagnosis, my husband had an incredible attitude about everything. Being a bit of a stoic, he praised God daily and accepted the cards he had been dealt. Early on, daily I seemed to be on a roller coaster between intense anger and crippling, unspeakable grief and loss. In time through much prayer, therapy, crying, reading, sharing, writing, meditation, yoga, running, and just showing up daily for life, we struggled through. Moments did come when both of us, individually and collectively began to experience joy. After almost two years, my husband was reevaluated and it seems that he did not have "classic" symptoms of Alzheimer's, dementia, or precognitive dementia, a precursor for Alzheimer's. At the family conference when we got this diagnosis, again, I was stunned stupid. I could not think clearly enough to say anything. When I did have questions others usually asked them, so I was a silent witness to a kind of miracle. Regardless of the diagnosis, he presented with kind some cognitive impairment, however. And, the biggest culprit was stress. Stress exacerbates everything. One of his nicknames was "Reverse Mike," so of course he did not have classic Alzheimer's. He still presented with mood swings – left water running and the stove on; forgot things; and repeated things twenty or thirty times as if he was saying it for the first time.

This wonderful, gentle bear of a husband, who was a genius, could still do miraculous things, and he taught me so much. He taught me to embrace serenity and to be intentional about reducing stress. Stress exacerbates Alzheimer's and many other diseases, especially hypertension, headaches, and weight gain. Bearing this reality in mind, we had to make major adjustments in how we related to each other. Our journey was so amazing, with some days resembling a roller coaster, difficult, up and down; challenging, painful, fearful, amidst desolation and futility. On some of these days, the dynamics clearly indicated that our combined struggle was not flesh and blood, but powers and principalities; harsh difficulties that were not generated by either of us, but by some powers that were clearly beyond our control.

Other days it was sweet communion, joyful sharing, and the quiet and peace of a delightful afternoon by the sea; laughter, teasing, fun. Taken together, there have been lots of lessons to learn, much misunderstanding, agony, anger, different realities, and pain, mixed in with joy, peace, and ultimately acceptance. We learned so much, and our walk with God and each other shifted.

Miraculously, Spring 2005 Mike got his mind back. He had taken himself off the statin drugs and the Alzheimer's drug, Aricept, the year before. He could feel when the drugs kicked in and when they were not doing anything. A year off these drugs, we truly experienced a miracle. One afternoon after I returned from work, Mike said, "By the way, when you said XYZ this morning. . ." I looked at him in shock and asked, "You remember what I said?" He paused and said, "Yes." Prayers were answered. Mike no longer presented as if he had Alzheimer's, classic or otherwise! Being the scholar he was, he researched and found out that many persons had had dementia like symptoms from taking statin drugs. An astronaut had a rare form of amnesia from taking statins. (So if your loved one or you ever present as if you have some type of cognitive disorder, especially the four that are related – Alzheimer's, Dementia, Parkinson's, and Loewy bodies, please check the medication, to see what the side effects are, and what type of contraindications relate to the drugs they or you take. With all that occurred over our last dozen years together, and the healing that God afforded us, it became apparent that the next step would be to share our story with others. Clearly, God called me to share this story as a way to helps others see, you may be down, but not out.

I have felt deep rage, disappointment, and grief; these feelings have permeated my skin and inhabited my innermost self. Electrified by rage and paralyzed by grief, I have known betrayal as loss; have been down, but never out; and, we have come through, doing life in different ways. I have gone from Ps. 22, "My God, My God, why have you forsaken me," through Is. 40:31, "They that wait upon the Lord, shall renew their strength, they shall mount up with wings like eagles; they shall run and not get weary; walk and not faint;" to Ps. 30:5, "Weeping endures for a night, but joy comes in the morning (mourning).

And so, I offer this work in memoriam to all those who have experienced deep anger, loss, and betrayal. Today, I embark each day, living one moment at a time, learning to not over commit, overwork; to have time to rest, write, and listen for God. The timing of committing these reflections to paper is a time of healing, celebration, and renewal. In creation itself, God undertakes a covenant experience with us, where our creation was pronounced good. Isn't all good ultimately rooted in God? God's magnificent creativity produced us. God created us for relationships, to embrace each other in love. Unrequited rage, angst, and all forms of negativity thwart love, diminish joy, and strangle our capacity to live in hope. The beauty of Genesis 1, the first creation story is that God created each one of us, in love, to embody love, to express love and admiration, and be in healthy relationships. The phrase, "God's don't make no junk," reminds us that every human being is a gift, and that with the quest for wellness and wholeness, we can maximize what God has given us, as we follow the adage of Jesus, "love the Lord your God with all your heart, and love your neighbor, as yourself: what a simple axiom, what a complex task. *Baptized Rage, Transformed Grief*, is a litany, a lived sermon, meditations as call and response, an invitation for us all, with the help of God, to create as stress free life as possible, while it is yet morning. Welcome to a life journey. I invite you to see yourself on the page and learn more about how to learn to be a healthy physical, mental, emotional, sensual, sexual, spiritual self.

Baptized Rage, Transformed Grief introduces the concepts of beginnings and context, rage and grief; portrays many sides of rage and resolves that anger or rage can be creative and is a choice; depicts grief and loss as an in-between place of anguish and pain that often follows anger, and precedes healing and completion. Such fury and sorrow also celebrate the journey through rage and grief toward hope, transformation, and an ultimate covenantal relationship with God. The experience of intense physical activity, working with cardiovascular exercises, doing weight training, and the hot yoga have provided openings to new insights in the realms of all of life. Half marathons and my first full marathon in 2010 were all celebrations of God's presence in my life, and in my relationships, particularly with Mike.

This volume ends with three poems written moments after Mike's death, in weeks following when betwixt and between incredulity, shock, sadness, anger, grief, fear, and hurt – flowed in and out, amid the knowledge of celebration and a need to let go. Much of who he was/is lives in me. I see the world differently, larger, more imaginatively, and with such a deep sense of gratitude. I miss him terribly. As he rests at Arlington National Cemetery, cradled in the arms of God, I know a peace that passes all understanding. I am moved and grateful to be able to unfold this experience in this volume, *Baptized Rage, Transformed Grief.*

Deserts, Wells, Stalactites

Your agony rages
deep below the bowels of your spirit
Right on the surface of your heart and mine
I ache to let you know I care:
My language seems too soft,
too confusing
I can't seem to get through.

You've cried out in deep pain
Some have come to bring safety;
Some seem not to understand
how dry this desert--
how depleted your well--
How moments are heartbeats of struggle:
We fight for your soul.

Confusion and complexity abound
Questions for information inadvertently echo skepticism
From the abyss, midst angst and anger
Words uttered in response
Deep hurt strung like stalactites in
Caves deep below the earth
This noon, do not glimpse the light of day.

Now, Before, Then/Later

Now

Need to rejuvenate
to resuscitate
Tired marrow, iron deficiencies
Exploding one's sensibilities
Stretching nerves
Too taunt, too aggravated
Pain erupts.

Nurture and solace
Equip one's soul
to stand the ebbs and flows
of seasons, bringing
Brutal rains and seismic spasms
Cloaked in realms of normalcy.

Before

Shadows looming
Here and there
Disconnects, disappointments
Left unspoken.

Expectations
Made, not made
Illusory collective sanction
The threads
Holding most of it together.

Then/Later

Who knows the time of sunrise next year
the time of equinox sans astronomy
Sequential events of all reality
Tend not to make themselves known,
before tomorrow, becomes yesterday.

Faith shrouds the mysteries
Sacredness and miracles;
We later report
we experienced
Unbeknownst to ourselves.

Whirling Rivers

Emotions, thoughts
Feelings sloshing about
Turbulence unfurled
Unleashed before the baptism
      by the fires of your angst.

Waves pressing in the sands
of time and memories
going back out to sea
Washing away brittle particles.

Grains of fear, doubt, control
with each ebb <u>and</u> flow
Old and new blend,
Yet separate themselves,
as the tides anoint the shore afresh.

Soaring

Suspended thousands of miles
within oceans of blue sky
Clouds skipping about
Nonchalantly, sunning themselves.

Bones weary, mental fatigue
Wraps around my eyes
washing away the vales of worry;
Oh, be super-careful
Monitoring every phrase
To not set you off.

The mental gymnastics,
Emotional calisthenics,
Heavy exhaustion--
Gravity settles somewhere
near one's solar plexus.

Growing together
Shattering icons of
Isolation, obsession, goals
Asking for what you need
in moments, then and now
Articulate one's neediness,
the other's art of control.

No Baptism, No Tears

      Diapers and smells of talcum powder
        don't clutter our laundry--
       not something we have to store.
     Pins, bottles, teeny tiny blankets
        Never don our laundry
Oh, breathtaking emptiness, anguish unfurled.

No pitter patter of little feet –
No cacophony of noises
or toys strewn on stairwells:
No evidence of little ones
Treading up close
Pulling my skirt tail;
No fount of blessing here.

Terrified of asking why not,
Believed for so long
Miracles emptied before their birth
No wellspring of fertility.

     Arid, empty spaces
     like desserts bereft of life.
     Can't cry no more,
     Can't long no more,
     Can't hope no more
     for the baptism that will never be.

Waters of the Deep

Grief pours forth from a soul
Seeps through pores:
Like thick, oozing pus
Foul smelling,
Setting off a duress
Somewhere from the depths of eternity
Ancestral wailing
Earth, herself groaning
Mourning the lives that never were.

Disbelief, angst, outrage
the arrogance, blatant disregard
What couldn't be birthed
Couldn't be conceived
Couldn't imagine us embracing
A life in our care.

How dare you?
Who made you God?
She sees babies and loving homes,
and her heart breaks.

The hurt goes back before time
before chaos
Before God moved
Over the deep,
And extends
into Eternity.

Torrential Rains

        If I cry
            The tears may never stop
    The inconsolable waters
        flowing profusely;
Storms, cloudbursts
            Raging within
    Awakening pain
           Niagara Falls unfurled.

If I cry

My soul exposed
Nerve endings electrified
great drops of liquid
from the ducts
Beneath my lashes
Shutters photographing
snapshots of incredulity
that do not disappear
When learned eyes
Partake their wonder
'Neath the mists,
no more sorrow
Irrupted from pain.

Dripping Anger

Rage, oozing from pores
Emerging deep from
Thousands of years
of collective, of individual suffering--
Evolved across oceans of torment
Coalescing in one body
Many bodies
Some vociferous
Some voiceless
Some forgotten
In old moldy documents
Decayed like the bodies
Living and dead depicted in print.

What drips from the epidermis
fails to cool
boiling chemicals rumbling
Just below the surface plains
Of I-amness.
Not cooling like perspiration
but burning like the acid
Produced below in caverns,
Molded by God, by time

To process food and water,
which cannot be, digested
which cannot make you well
In the disrupted chemical reading
Indicating volcanic-like
thoughts and memories
Indisposed to rest.

Baptized Rage

Listening to sermonic machinations:
Grounded midst enthusiastic piety
Family loyalty, communal civility
Antagonized my sensibility
of right and wrong.

        Good intent
        Charaded as law, gospel, and love
        Droned on betwixt
        "Amen's" and heads nodding
        served to stoke the ire just 'neath
        One's solar plexus
        Fueling dismay, disgust, disbelief
        And yes some judgment . . .

Disbelief at how right sounding words
are wrong
Dismay that misinformation
receives applause
Disgust at reductionism run amok_
Sadness that texts get misappropriated
That miseducation can be so blatant,
and that folks really believe the incorrigible of God!

Angry Cells, Skewed Waters

Cancer
The Big C
Riddles her organs
Fluid-filled lump
Like a cold, like a flu, like an allergy
A malaise that would not go away
Cells going berserk - - Big B: BAD
Big C - - out of control
Misbegotten tissues
Escalated Genesis
Creating no peace, havoc!

Vital water, necessary water
Can't, won't extinguish the fiery expanse
boiling beneath her epidermis--
Pain too intense for the
intricate, fragile, dainty--
Pain congealed by disbelief
Pain shocking into despair
A turn from what was, to what is, and will be
She's staggered along trajectories
of fear, hope, and finitude.

"Mists of Fury": Predatory Unfurled

Insult, injurious gestures
Perpetrated
by a Predator: poignant, unassuming
Facade of inquiry, curiosity
feigned desire to learn and grow
A shroud cloaking the intent
To seduce
To sate lust
Towards orgasmic mists
dampening sexual fury
satisfying perceived need
Be not too proud
Be not too naïve
To see the predator unfurled,
Witnessed before your actual face
Calling you to sleep with your enemy:
Rush *not* into a volcano
Hot lava hills,
Where you shall surely die.

Angered Sweat

Heart beating fast, too fast
Not quite palpitations
Breath ragged
Each chest movement
Telegraphing the rage, the disgust
At the despicable lies, bitching, condescending
Tone, lies, and innuendoes
Carved out on paper as gesture.

Heart still beating fast
Glands kicking in
Body working to cool itself
Cool the righteous indignation
As the water and salt mixes
Trickled from pores much alive- -

Rivulets working to wash away
Personal insanity and disrespect
Calling on Holy Spirit
For moistened, glorious reach
To remind one, who one is, and whose one is
Imploring personal prayer for reprobates
To pity their unremarkable lives - -
So crippled, that they have
To eviscerate others, before taking flight.

Fiery Puddles

Pools of water
Strewn about the cosmos
Are life-giving or life denying
When we honor or defile creation
Appreciating or tainting
the aesthetics of responsible love
Dispelled when grief and anger abound.
Weighty tears, falling
Filling the puddles
as they swell to become rivers.

Bitter Tears

Lashing out in words
To one he need not target
Became his smog of grief
For all the pain still within,
His frustration, meek bitterness
From lack of understanding
Permeated the conversation
Enumerating the angst, the disappointment
The troubled sensibilities

About communities that failed to respond –
Seeming in this moment
At once irrelevant
Simultaneously, having an impact
not hearing truth
Not feeling the joy, the release
of liberating tears.

Disappointed Streams

Tears streamed down her broken face
Ritualized pain and angst
above an empty womb
A cavern replete with the capacity
To be in process.

To engage, attach itself
to her body
Bringing new life
Renewal, reconnection, transitions
Multiplying generations
Creating more, extended families.

Potential, there since birth
Seems a reality that may not
Will not come to pass - -
Short a gargantuan miracle - -
Not to say such cannot happen
Just to say that her giving birth
Is highly unlikely.

Her pain is like the Titanic
Her anger is the rage of Vesuvius
Her sadness parallels teardrops of the oceans
Her hope, that light of a distant candle
Her disappointment - - an ever flowing stream
Rolling, rolling to a river
Flooding over from time to time.

Addictive Waters

Loss: emptiness plunged
beneath the catacombs of desire
Gross aches, disappointments, pain
Unresolved, misconstrued experiences
move us back to now
unless so trapped by yesterday
so fearful of tomorrow
We forget to live in the present.

Ragged Rain

Soft, slow droplets
Hydrogen and oxygen
Cascading from the skies
Oozing from her heart:

Angst and tears
Ancient yet now, new
Mirrors to one's psyche
Journeys in moments
Profound, inspiring avenues
a venture, preposterous
Encapsulated beyond
The boundaries of their dreams
About reality.

Damned Spot

Water spots, drops of blood
something dripped, something wasted
From pots and cups and hoses;
From veins and cuts and bruises
Signaling opened orifices
Challenging the reality of life itself.

Spitting out
Enraged at a friend's proclivities
to spend, spend, spend
Hoping to throw up guilt
To camouflage the fact
That spending so much
Of self and resource--

On STUFF
When self is depressed
And resources are tight
Makes other gestures
of reform and change
Mute, moot
A mirage,
Where the HOPE?

Agitated Monsoons

The vicissitudes of life
smacked them in the face
as they heard the litany
of their failings.

The embodied voice
Droned on with alacrity
Litigating in that very moment
the plaintiff's case
Impassioned pleas for self-care
Self-respect, mutuality, and dignity.

The well-being and certainty
of those who listen and speak
Engage the dialogical rhythms
of present time, molded by past hurts.

Mesmerize the consciousness
Images, sensations of now and then
Twirling together - -
The awakenings unfurling unprecedented turbulence.

We pray
the Eye of the storm
Passes over--
Death to things dead and toxic
Life to things living and new.

Ragged Dewdrops

Life in petri dishes
on slides
Microbes: vile, destructive organisms
Wretched...parasitic clusters of death targeted
Escalated organic processes
Vulnerable life forms
Potency, immeasurable--
Beyond the pale of safety
Squelching all bents of invincibility
Ragged, torn, poisonous innuendoes
Rest, like dew on the surface of one's soul.

The Strain

Defeated --
No! Tired, exhausted
from the on-going analysis
Creating a quasi-paralysis
of the spirit:

A wounded heart
A scapegoating symphony
for all the wrongs,
The misfits
The communicative rhythms
That don't quite work:

Expansive --
Exponential
One sigh
Signifying the weariness
of ten thousand ages
Tempered by
those powers Everlasting
Desiring the El Dorado
of peace, and contentment.

In the moment
Shedding the garments of fatigue:
Spiritual, mental, emotional.

If but for a moment
Sixty seconds of joy
Like a cochlear implant
affording hearing,
and listening in new ways
Scaling the dams of
Depression, rage, fear, betrayal, angst --
If but for the time it takes
To sip a cup of tea.

The Heavy Feet

Lead weighted their bodies
and their souls and minds.
Even their heavy feet could not
help them stand up against reality.

Burdens of truths
Unimaginable
attached themselves
like leeches
That could suck out
the poisons from her blood.

How long, how much?
How could the heavy feet
Help them sustain the continuous agony
the onslaught of violence of disrespect
The denial of their humanity
The fear over against rage
Mixed, shaken, not stirred
In the martinis/stews/casseroles of injustice.

Missed Thoughts

                        Grief weighted their bodies
                        their souls and minds.
                        Each breath pained
                        their internal vessels
                        like bellows pressing back life,
                        As it seemed to seep away.

              The thoughts
        Banged like an anvil chorus
           Hammering, ringing
       Louder that the diapasons
         on the greatest organs
           as they whimpered
         Knowing the magnitude
         the stamina it would take
When the doors, their minds, their eyes:
    the windows would open no more.

Realizing that that will be then,
And this is now
They rejoiced for another few seconds,
Perhaps days, months, a year or two or three?
Maybe,
Of their lovers gentleness
That wrapped around souls connecting;
But only if they forgot about tomorrow
And lived their best today.

Overwhelm

Overwhelm
Danced about the surfaces
of their flesh
Piercing the realm of mystery, of spirit
of heart and emotional sensibility.

Caught in a sea of reality
The spirit weeps for solitude;
for peace, and clarity.
Waves of tumult
Drown out joy;
Who will remember to ask:
"Where are the life preservers?"

Has faith gone asleep?
Is it dormant?
Where doth hope go
when hopelessness abounds?
Does faith, juxtaposed against deep pain
indicate pity or trust?

Wet from the deluge
Of tormented reality;
Oceans turn to many tears;
The release,
Leaving an emptiness,
A quiet,
A stillness, a sign:
Spent, beyond exhaustion - - - - - -
Weary of the circumstances,
Grateful for the journey.

Clouds Dancing

Wisps of vapor
Suspended above earth
separately, spaced, penetrable.
Light and plane soar through
as colder air now
makes their independence jaded.
More ambiguity and uncertainty
Metamorphosed in seconds.

Clouds, like a fleet of ships
Poised for adventure
Shift not when cool air surrounds
and like cotton balls
will joy abound?
Suspended, as their shadows touch earth.
The cool mists disappear
Signally, God spoke yesterdays
God speaks today.

Signifying resignation and acceptance
Despite pain and suffering, public and private--
Informs me that we do not need to
Ask "why?"
Know why!
Embracing the gift of today
A quest for peace
Beyond stress.

Steaming Rage

Teapot
Boiling over; too hot to pour
Water from its spout
for steam
Scalds and burns
Like words vitriolic.

Spewing forth
Wrapped in turmoil
signifying "my way or else"
Trapped beneath the pain
Locked within.

Steam swirling
Its mist permeating air and space
without boundaries
without need
Can melt, can burn
Can dissipate
Does it disappear
Or morph into something else?

Pissed Ire

Sweat dripping
Furrowed brow
Consciousness of breath – ahh, ahh –
Panting, sensual sighs – kick girl, kick boy, run–

Salty drops
Cooling their bodies
Steaming like molten lava
As they rehearsed reflections
Of ire and rage:
with life's rough moments
Feigned expectations

Disappointments
Hurt feelings
People dying too soon
Kick – kick – top of the hill –
Up, up, past stop sigh; run/walk

Downhill - - yes –
A little prayer...another quarter mile
More sweat
More release
Home – stretch – shower
A calmness
Ire dissipated:
For the moment.

Tormented Downpour

The words stung
like the shocks one gets when
Electricity kicks back.

The impact of the words fell
like a blinding downpour
too dense and intense;
too wet to afford sight,
the seeing
of what's so.

How wet, chilling, painful
for the core of marrow
Someday to ashes, they become--
Yet as the heart doth beat.

Dutifully, on schedule
Regulating life, moment to moment - -
iced fear and trembling
Transferred to our being
became a disruptive force;
at once, paralyzing.

Though framed by a spiritual knowledge
that appearances torment,
may or may not be the reality
Meted out through a chain of words:
Numbed by in-depth aching
Riveted with sadness, loss, and grief
Yet, framed and heard
In covenant and hope.

Dripping Pain (Anguish, Angst

Caldrons of lava
Beneath the Geospheres
      of time and self
Affords a disconnect
A denial, not even that - -
But an awareness of molten lava
That quivers below
Terrains of consciousness

In times of eruption
From deep below one knows
Not the volcanic ash
The heat, the agony
Of self and the one
Who may experience
The contentions, the strains
Of spewing molten rock—

For other surfaces
Know not this rage
And know only the
Shining of the sun.

Putrid Fog

The filthy smell of anger
Viewed as negative
Stifled the creativity
The spontaneity of the heart
Ordained by God.

Scented candles and incense
Failed to cloak the waning vomit
Wafting forth
in the dark atmosphere
of depression and dysfunctionality.

The drops of codependence
With the clouds of confusion and discontent
Produced a fog
Dense with feelings
Acknowledged and denied.

Anger, like fat, when burned
When viewed positively
Smells sweet
And becomes an offering to God.

Engorged Pools

Rapid heartbeats
Pulsing, banging
Against cages
Of bone, nerves, tissues
Chime out the angst
of the moment.

Like ants
on maneuvers
Moving, moving, moving
Scurrying over
Old and new territories
Signifying life
Embodying concern
Hoping to escape worry –

And then
A new reality
A calculation
Dismay, wonderment, FEAR
Regret, surprised reality
Who/what wants to turn off your light?

Pools of thoughts
Like molecules in ponds
Which in your mind
In hope against malady
As spirit and thought
Go to war for sanity
For serenity
For serendipity,
in anticipation.

Tearful Hurt

Injustice
Riddles our realities
When people die too soon.
When great minds become incapacitated
When pompous idiots make bad decisions
that affect who we are.

Pain wells up
Responding to the anguish
Framing the episodes
       of self, community, life
Embracing the many continuums of life and death - -
The moment to moment
Realities that flood our awareness.

Tearing against, eating away
Those parts of us, vulnerable
to circumstance, age, health, economics, all oppression
Tears of recognition
Loss, grief, pain
are the prelude to the never of now.

Thunderous Insanity

Rumbling noises
Bombarding one's sensibilities
Noises so frightening
Causing one's skin to goose up
The hair on my neck to stand
so jarring these noises of life
so rapidly they come - -
Yearning for peace and serenity.

Cacophony unleashed
As storms rage
        Winds blow
A symphonic night
        shattering the interludes
of momentary respite
When sleep comes

Like tympanis and kettle drums
Low pulses of sound resonating
        Echoing the ruminations of life
Coursing through my veins;
Life smells skipping through my nostrils
Conglomerates of pixels I see before me.
Your love ever surrounds me.

Ruptured Fluids

Long ago, crying so hard
Tears flooded so - -
that he could cry no more.
no tears could he shed
when his beloved,
when they were left void
an emptiness
caused by God, the abortionist
who deemed they would not
have a child.
not through their communion
nor through adoption.

When their souls did meet and create,
the impulse of life
that died at 7 weeks:
The pain intense
The loss - - deep;
The anguish indefinable
The divine betrayal astronomical.

          And he ate his pain
          to be there for her - -
          there are no reasons why,
          any reasons given
          are inconsequential
          to the devastation,
          the disappointment

          The dismal reality:
          when a naked womb
          an empty placenta

> exacted ruptured fluids:
> dry tears
> dead fetus in useless tissue

The signification of
unfulfilled dreams
thwarted hopes
unheard cries
the absence of progeny
a disconnect with
generations never to come.

We won't receive
the blessings of Abraham
(Genesis 12:1-3)
the covenant God made:
promises of an heir.
Did God lie?

Liquid Agony

25 Pounds of Pain
Signifies the need to
"Lay aside every weight,"
A scripture of wholeness
Riddled with a wisdom
That often escapes
Our frail, human sensibilities.
A divine word - -
For many occasions.

Weight embraces:
Deep fears paralyzing
Joy and life in the moment
Hopeless regret galvanizing
Unconscious awareness - -
      Depleting glandular reserves;
Traumatizing anger
Twisting the soul
      Into Gordian's Knot.
      Insatiable sadness
The depths of which
There is no measure.

Renegade thoughts:
The what if's
The used to's, ought to's
Should have's, would have's
That died before
Their essential nature
Took flights of fantasy

Thus, weighted down,
The integrated soul/mind/body
Has no option –
But to show signs
Of Heaviness, bloating:
Of dis-ease.

Baptized Rage: Grief Reconciled

Running faster, harder
Running from and through
The demons of anger
Nipping at her ankles
Her heart, her soul
Binding a weightiness
Where freedom's desired.

She ran faster, faster
Sweat, forming pools
        On her brow
Kickin' butt
Going many miles –
Running, running
Through and away from
Anger? Maybe?
Pain – yes!
What kind: grief

A grief so deep
As to crown God
With a dunce cap.
A grief so profound
She could taste the Bitterness

As she swallowed
A grief so traumatic
That no diets –
No exercise
Gave her body permission
To "lay aside the weight"
Weight

Her body had manufactured
To grab her attention
To tell her
Something was/is wrong –
A grief
Connected to all
Mourners throughout time.
A wailing so loud
As to drown out
And obliterate
A sonic boom.
Transformed (grief)

Volcanic Rain

Her God consciousness
Ever present
A sense of comfort and certainty
An assurance anchoring her
Ancestors as long as memory
        radiated her being
Became shaken
When learning that God
      was not answering her
      prayer in this life.

Used, Abused, Discarded

Woke up, stretched
Hit the day running, realized
They had used me
Want to use me up (abuse)
Then get all mystified
      As to why I'm not going to be
      their puppet any more.
One more loss
One more thing to grieve
They've abused and discarded me
Worse yet
They've discarded my dreams –
Another stroke of creativity
Dissipated thru lack of vision
      Angst and jealousy of others
Wearied from their own drudgery
Not caring a whole lot
      About mine.

The Grief Cycle

Grief 1

Knowing his mind is disappearing
Drifting away
That his encyclopedic mind
One day may not recognize his own name
Shakes my entire being
Like a .9 on the Richter scale.

The mental, brilliant discourses will cease
The ability to care for others will be no more
The beingness
        ontology and existential presence
As lover, friend, confidante, editor, pal
        husband, cheerleader, bed partner
        house spouse, church worker
        12-step mentor, Dad, good guy all disappear
Even in this moment
I know a deep sense of loss; a cavernous emptiness

Grief 2

Terror crept down my spine
And gripped my heart.
As I see your brilliance
Seeping away from your grasp
Fear floods my soul.
I shudder, because you'll be here
And simultaneously you'll not be here –
My foundation is being shaken
In ways I couldn't imagine.

Grief 3

Mournful mists
Flood over the bay
As heavenly waters weep
For things that never will be again

Mists cannot warm the dull, dull sensibility
Resident amid the places of the heart
And spirit
Where pulses still occur
Beating, pumping
In the stillness what

Cities of regret
Rivers of what if's
States of unrest
Signifying a low wail
Whose angst is unmeasurable.

Angry Waters

"Baptism"
Pouring, swirling
Round my ankles
Rivulets profound: sand and water
Shifting salty sand and water
Blurring boundaries
Removing certainty
Ambiguity the norm.

Elements moving
Earth revolving
Questioning what's so?
Interrogating reality
Things we label important
Evaporatingly insignificant
They are no more.

Amidst the waters: release
"In the name of the Creator": swooosh
Rumbling seas, Ocean massive
Ancient cries resound from the deep,
"In the name of Christ": Ahhhh -- --- --
Particles shifting beneath my being
Sea and sky connected.
"In the name of the Holy Spirit": Ssssh -- -- --
Letting go of heartache for generations
Injustices, systemic and otherwise
I resist, re-know in the present
My baptism.
Recommit my life to incarnated Love, justice, and community
In solidarity with: many thousands gone

Cargo from Middle passage
Conquered from Vieques*
With myself.

Musings before Noon

Clock, tick tock, tick tock --
What is time, that it controls
The onus of now --
the possibility of what may never be
Ruminating over angst, anger, agitation
That seeks to bubble up this morning,
from some nether region
so deep and far away that it seems
unreal and imaginary.

Yet the imaginary lurks
just below the epidermis
Wanting to explode, to lash out, and then
the voice of sanity
cloaks the realm of tenuous insanity
And with breathing comes perspective;
And with perspective comes quiet;
And with quiet comes balance;
And with balance
comes renewed vision and focus on today.

And the gift of today
Is the gift of now;
Is the release of yesterday
Is to abandon worry about tomorrow;
Is to be present
And open
And vulnerable.

For the facts and feelings of now;
And now may become was;
And now may become then.

And if now becomes was or then
It is no longer now
And the muddling of time
Often nurses
Children of regret, fear, and resentment:
A formula antithetical
to peace and contentment;
A recipe for disaster, unless
The moment becomes opportunity to be;
To trust God = relying on God for the results
And to abandon the need to control:
An idolatrous practice of distorted desire.

And so waiting on God
Becomes an opportunity to be in this moment
Hopeful; asking question, praying;
taking action
Letting go,
Releasing others to themselves
Tapping into acceptance of what is:
Remembering to breathe;
Remembering
To not take self or anyone too seriously.
Remembering to laugh and dance
A shift in energy
A shift toward Grace embodied:
My higher power, who when I listen
Answers questions in fascinating ways.

Numbed Silence

Sitting, I weep inside
Even as tears seem not to want to fall
My body cries, though my eyes remain dry
In the throes of a deep pain
Hovering about my toes
No skipping along near my heart.
which beats normally on a physical plane
Beats too slow on a spiritual plane
As part of me that never got born
Has already died in life, but not in my mind.

I weep now for you, my child
Who I will never hold
Never scold, or teach alphabets
And sing songs to you
Like my parents sang to me.

You will never be born, my little one
Never shall I suckle you at my breast
And run behind you as you move along on unsteady legs
As you learn to ride a bicycle
Perhaps play your first recital
Your first tennis or soccer match
Perhaps bake your first cake
Engage your first computer program
Or any other firsts that may have been
And never will they be.

My heart aches
For pictures I can never show
For dates on the calendar I will never write
For religious rituals we will never participate in

For graduations that will never happen
For the adult conversations that we can never have
Oh, God, my soul aches
How could this be, that such a blessing
Never occurred?
Oh, I mourn for those who have longed like I --
I pray for all those who have this void
That someday will know a sense of "it's OK."
And now my beloved, the tears fall
like rain on a gentle summer morn
for my defenses are down
And until I can release this pain
I cannot go forward.

Stunned Grief

Rousing from the deep sleep of night
Hearing an indictment
Sank deep within the spirited persona of self
Impaled at the stake
Devastated beyond belief
That the conviction of cruelty to another
Had been pronounced.

Love the sinner and hate the sin
Proved no consolation --
Attributing the comparison with cruelty,
bully, self-centered, obsessive compulsive
Pierced the core of reality
As if a nuclear fission occurred.

The denotation
Shook the foundations of the moment
To such a deep place
One could only be racked by tears
For to even repeat those utterances
Vile upon the ears
Was too demoralizing to imagine.

With the injunction to not moralize
To give witness to what was spoken
As intervention
Riveted to an awareness of possibility
With deep regret.

The option now is to seek truth
To face those truths
To embark on the tightrope
Naked before God
In search of the holy grail of self knowledge
Wading amidst deep grief
Toward the other side.

Wet Grief

Grief smothered me like a wet blanket;
Dampness infused with the musty,
        dank fragrance of dreams unrequited
And then the Almighty touched me:
        a gentle breeze kissed my soul,
As the uncomfortable covering became
        a waterfall of tears;
            Welling up from the bowels of my soul:
Graced moments in the present
A declaration of my pain held too tightly
        as Grace slipped in and bided its time
            as my weary spirit shook: sobs became ancient wails of woe.

And in minutes, the moisture of gentle tears
Warmed my heart
as a testimony to let go,
and let God, and be in the now --
Burying the dead that at one point
had refused to die.

Cruel Madness

The words
The inflections
The negation of us;
of reality,
Cut deep into the
Vicissitudes of being.

The pain so immediate
the sorrow unnerving
the angst riveting
Nonbeing, trapped by awareness.

Since safety for the wounded is gone
and total wellness is no more
Projection and replication
Becomes the order of the day
Empathy run amuck.

What is left is what is –
The insanity of another
Confronted me today.
Stared me down
Smacked me stupid
But, I'm still standing.

Fainting Mists

The ravages of loss
like tentacles from
some giant crustacean reached out –
and nulled memories,
abilities to recall to learn anew;
These gifts
snatched away
Before the next decade
Unfurled before us.

Awareness, cognition, retention
Seeping away
like flour in a sifter
Shifting like sands
in an hour glass
Dripping down
into cavernous places
of no return.

Such awakening
Puts my heart in check
Wounds deeply
Squelching,
What is –

Yet, yesterday is a mist
an experience important then –
We know not how many tomorrows
loom amid consciousness –
We grieve the dissipation
and we embrace this moment
The moment of now;
And give thanks for
the Consciousness and love of this hour.

Bastardly Betrayal

And her heart, crushed
by the weight of knowing
the Epistemic reality that what is
Is, and will not change, and
will only get worse
and will only hurt more
and will not go away
until death unlocks the door
of forgotten memory.

And little things
at once seem trivial
and in that same second,
embody the weight of the world.
Big things that need to get accomplished
Hang on 'til the twelfth of never
Can't get the focus
And the energy together
To be the usual disciplined self
For the betrayal
Stood up and
Knocked her down
In a way
That made it hard to get up –
At points to even believe she could get up.

But her faith held her, even still
And she knew the prayers of her friends
were holding her, even as her spirits wilted
And her hopes daunted
For the thirteenth moment
Seemed frozen
As her awareness was so raw
As to be excruciatingly painful
That loving you
Could hurt so much
For all the right reasons.

And so
In this moment of now
Perhaps the tears will stay at bay
For she must be about other tasks
Before day becomes night
becomes day yet again
As her weeping may come for nights and many days to come
But love, in the moment
Can be that balm in Gilead.

Death: Just a Breath Away

Life and death,
Point and counterpoint
Face-off each moment:
between inhale and exhale.

Between each breath we take,
People live,
People die.
Life comes;
Death takes no holiday,
Death visits:
Noisily, quietly, repulsively, peacefully, enigmatically—
Where did all that hot air go?

Butterflies fly,
 Death comes.
 Praise, Adore, Embody God:
 Live life.
 Die, dead, expire.
Death for me, death for you
When we let oppression
Snuff out our life force:
our ideas, our actions,
Our very being:
Gloria in Excelsis Deo!
Our essence
Exits stage left.
We allow
Things and people
to break our sweet communion
with God,
Unadulterated theft.

Revolutionary Revelation

Midst yoga practice--
Sweating, twisting, breathing – somewhere
between fixed firm and rabbit poses,
Spirit spoke to me saying
"Your Anger fuels your skin cancer!"

And I realized that
My first skin eruption
That which was diagnosed para-psoriasis
and Medics not sure what causes this ailment
and no cure for it --
        was precipitated by a professor's callousness
        Steeped in his mental illness, societal racism and sexism --
        There was no institutional support;
Yet I knew my call to complete the doctoral program
Was divinely sanctioned, a divine requirement
And I was committed --
So I pressed through.

Across the years, other life issues caused pain
        premature deaths, disappointments, betrayals
And sometimes my response was rage, anger:
the cloak, language, litany, and ritual
Of my deep pain and injury.

The list is long:
        Failure to conceive;
        conception gone amuck after seven weeks, dead fetus
        Failure to adopt:
        social worker bias against mixed race, brilliant couple with too
much faith;
        Oppression in the work place

        disrespect, jealousy
        sexism, manipulation, control
        false accusations, insufficient funds, racism
    Disappointment, expectations, blaming;
    Chaos around money, relationships, communication, blame from others;
    The stuff of life, where pain emerges
    And sometimes unbeknownst to me,
was addressed by, coped with, unconscious, automatic, autonomic response -- rage.

As skin is my largest organ
And now with this awareness
I deeply want this angst processed and gone;
And now at acceptance
I vow in this moment
To let go, and let God,
That I may be healed.

Mental Aerobics

Something was lurking around the rooms,
the salons within my head.
Realizing powers and principalities, adversarial
       thoughts were having a field day
Armed with pen and breath
Pen to chronicle throats and feelings
Breath to be grounded and connect with
Divine elegance.

And I remembered
Emotions are--
It is OK to have them.

Moving about like a whirling dervish
My job = seeking joy over burdens
Is to stay right with God
Do the next right thing
Trust God for the results
Laugh lots
Hit reset button;
So I press on, and let God handle the rest.

Starved for Rest

Busted, bloated, blessed
In meditation, God reminded me--
Mind, body spirit all one
Busted on notions that any
one part of us, rocks and rules
Our realities are like a
symphony, life is an orchestral work
Needing winds, brass, percussion, and strings.

Bloated from lack of sleep
And from eating something
That shouted out inside;
We're not feeling this--
Bloated from fatigue and misery
Blessed to know God and to be mindful about prayer
and work and twelve steps – all good
Blessed to know change is real and gift.
Blessed, I don't' have to stay stuck.

Exposed Canvases

Vulnerability beads up
Like perspiration on the face of a runner:
Trickling down from armpits moving, moving forward --
The sweat of ancient labor revisited
Weighted on the backs of slaves,
of immigrants deemed other
Of first nations peoples who
honor the Grace of land and place.

Vulnerability escalates
a beating heart, to palpitations
a breathing lung, to hyperventilation
Critical moments of nakedness
On the vast abyss of time and need
Painting vast strokes of fear
Of mystery, of the unknown
On exposed canvases of life.

Vulnerability offers
Opportunities for a renewal of faith
for a deepened appreciation for what is
In the elegance of rain
The dancing of fire
The gyrations of wind
The lashing tongues of fire
Elements that provide
that make manageable
The gift of life that we live.

Despairing Hues of Night

Despair settles down
Like a blanket, too comfortable
that clings to my body,
Perfectly fitting the contours and turns of my torso.
As wistful I sit,
Knowing that night has now come
and I must simply be with myself
For no other alternative
Avails itself in this wretched moment..

When morning became day and noon and afterwards
This cloak hung so loosely 'round my shoulders
that the gifts of camaraderie, laughter, and possibility
Soared like shooting stars about the galaxy.

And when night came:
I wondered if the day had been but a dream
For the stories at midnight were cloudy
Filled with tragedies dancing about
Mocking my notions of civility
Foisting fatigue upon me
As pillars of the lost continent, Atlantis.

Yet, somewhere beyond the recesses
Of all that is devastatingly despicable
Resounding of discordant melodies
Bounces a glimmer of hope
that something about all of this
Must get better
For I must breathe.

To breathe is to live;
To breathe is to be vital;
To breathe signifies possibility
Breath connects us with God.

Weighted by Fatigue

Fatigue
Washed in
as ocean waves
across the sands of time,
Shifting the seemingly
Solid mass:
Granules of earth
Moving about your toes
as the muddy bottom
Fails to anchor your body.

                                            Saturated in reality
                                              Wandering midst;
                              Gray clouds with scarred linings
                                        blocking the rays
                                        that could illumine
                                      But fail to refract
                            Illumination embedded within:
                                Weighted by life incidents
                                    Corseted by relevancy.

Fatigue Revisited toward Love

Fatigue
Pours out of my eyelids
as tears fall,
Washing my soul afresh
Extolling my cavernous grief
Knowing that you will be gone.

Fatigue and loss
Like a fugue
Reiterating the same motif
in various patterns
Sometimes with prelude
Sometimes with knowledge
of ultimate resolution
Reminds me of your, of our date
With your death.

Yet anchored in faith,
Knowing I must pray and praise
Rooted in the wisdom and
hope of my ancestors
I remain steadfast!
Holding on, grasping,
standing on God's promises--
Even when numb, or at peace
at surrender, at acceptance.

In the moment of now
The is-ness of it all saturates the marrow
Where life lives and dies
Facing life and death
Contemplating how best
To celebrate with you
Your gift of life
By God to you and me
Knowing the noise of life's stuff
That tends to impede.

In this moment as I breathe,
I see your face and your smile
and hear your low, rumbling laugh
And emblazon these experiences
On my heart for when you are gone.

And for now you are here
And I give thanks
And I cherish these moments
I cherish you as life itself
For you are life
Bigger than life
as your heart
Is so huge and gives so much:
Thanks for sharing
your heart with me.

Speaking, Listening, Loving, Living

Speaking
becomes surrealistic
Commitments and promises
and desires seem to get suspended
As the communication ends in pain.

                Unconditional listening
                gets trapped in response
          Triggers launched, buttons pushed
               Makes what then unfolds
                  Seeming impossible.

Feeling attacked, one stiffens
The formerly, quieted rage
Emerges, one's feelings hurt
The other's feelings hurt
  A truce needed.

                Expectations bounce around
                    More hurt feelings
                   Colors of red, orange
                colors of grey, midnight blue
                  Pain ripples everywhere
How can we get this roller coaster to stop?

How can I listen; unconditionally
That even when I'm baited
I come from a point of love.
God grant me peace;
Peace, unimaginable
Help me to exude peace
At every moment
Help me not to react from pain
Help me not to need to be right
Help me to come from acceptance.

                Help him have a will to live.
                I'm so tired, weary, in pain;
                I don't know what to do
                I show up for support groups
                Make phone calls
                Go to therapists
                Listen to you, to others
                and the few gracious moments
                Seem to end in a barrage of accusations.

                                Thanks yous, and appreciation
                                Get stamped down by
                                rhetoric of condemnation
                                Comparisons abound
                                Jesus, we give it all to you.
                                Fix me Jesus; fix my heart
                                Fix my pain. Fix me.

Questions, Interrogations

I don't know
When I've felt so
Down and out
So beaten
So helpless
So overwhelmed
So misunderstood
So interrogated
So sad
In such pain.

Crises and hard times
Shake our very foundations
In the midst
Of chaos, pain, loneliness
Danger, hard times.

Where is my faith?
Asleep, perhaps
With me all the time
Holding me so that
I do not break?

Where is my love
of God, of me, of others?
Should not love
cloak me, shield me
In a way that
Brokers resilience?

Should not faith and love
Together create
an elasticity, a bond
a certainty
That affords
an experience of Grace
That the fire's not so hot as to scorch--
The ice not too cold to freeze
Who and where am I?

I'm hurting
I'm angry
I feel betrayed by God,
By many others--
I'm tired of :
Being interrogated every day
Being made wrong
Being undermined
Being doubted
Being projected upon
Being stressed out.

Yoga Moments

        Yoga moments
        Open, vulnerable
      Air rushing in and out
      Muscles taunt, rippling
    Mind empirical towards *ruach*
      Soul totally exposed.

    Sun flowers
        strong, radiant, spectacular
      remind me of hope and opportunity
    of vibrancy
as the tears trembling
    Behind my eyelids
      Pronounce
        The raw relevance of pain
      Resilience of God's love within
    Revelatory nature of
One's beingness
    One's existential mystery
      Shaped by folk, feelings, freedom.

        In this moment before
      Immersion into body, mind, spirit
      Breath, sweat, determination
          mingling--
  an early morning breakfast soup
  The acknowledgement of grief
  and sadness rest in my bosom
  Nestled between my breasts
Socio-biological indicators of womanhood.

As I witness the depths
The cavernous valleys of
sadness, loss, disappointment
Resonating in my viscera, my DNA.

In these intense moments of new realities
Awash with ambiguity and uncertainty
I look inside and beyond for hermitage;
for refuge and sanctuary.

Problems Hovering

Problems overwhelm my environs
I am not problematic;
Not demonic, not bad
Shaken, torn; yet resilient

If I can speak my truth
And you speak your truth
And we can embrace
One another in love
Perhaps we can begin, again.

Acid Boiling

Nausea
Boiling, trembling,
Like a washing machine
System unbalanced
Breath rapid
Oooooooh, breathe.

Come Spirit:
Hold me, as things fall apart
amidst conflict, static
Viscera unsettled.
What's inside wants to
Push out, the physical self
the nausea unrelenting.
Though I just did my Sabbath exercise
there's still unsettledness
The emotional overrides
the mind, spirit and body:
I am here, where I am.

Not elated
Not defiant
Just sick
In Kierkegaardian terms
"With fear and trembling;"
"Sick unto death!"

Acid Boiling

I breathe
I take in more breath
Sweat dripping
Heart slowing
Nausea shifting--
Like Fannie Lou Hamer
Noted Civil Rights activist:
"I am sick and tired of being . . . tired;"
of being flummoxed
of being prodded and pushed
of being questioned and doubted.

I come back into this moment
Less nauseous, weary
Believing that, with discovery
Comes healing.

Sweet Dreams

Tired and content
I sigh at the awesomeness of the day,
And the conundrums and the cacophonous laughs
at my beloveds strange
funny, humorous jokes --
That delight my heart,
And soothe my weariness
And brings joy within
And phenomenal peace.
I know when sleep comes this night
a deep rest will embrace
My heart, my soul, my body
Honoring a blessed, beautiful day
Where we labored in love
To communicate, to share, to be
Together we grow in Grace
In God, in blessedness
In beauty,
I say good night.

Many Days before Christmas

Out in nature,
Running, feeling great
And God spoke
And told me why
The pitter, patter of tiny feet
of my womb, of his heart, our souls
Never came to pass:

This could not happen

God deemed it could not
Too many concerns between the two of us;
Physical, mental, emotional
       healing to happen
Other people's children to help
To teach, to love, to mentor, to care for --
And he had already begotten seven times
And so my womb dormant
       after a miscarriage
Two soul(s) that couldn't be born--
And now, I pray to accept
What at one time had been unacceptable.

God says no, and said "I'm sorry,"
       for your disappointment.
And now I must grieve;
and then some moment;
at some time, fully let go
And watching kids in the holiday program
Brings tears.

My heart, breaking, realizing
time has come to embrace a new reality.
        A time that has never been.
In this moment this time
will never be, Can never be.

And so I mourn – the times of never
Gifts wrapped today were
for other people's children;
children and grandchildren
I'm connected with; not of my bloodline.
This pain – palatable
Present against my being
has shaken my reality
My desire is to be in the present
To embrace acceptance,
        moment by moment.
And if or when I stay
        in the moment
Grief will be my companion
Though not for too long --
As long as need be--
And that's OK.

I believe the anger is gone;
Disappointment lurks around the fringe
Not so powerful as before.
With this new awareness
has come a kind of numbness
A clarity in the mind space
A trembling ache in the heart space
A quiet voice in the spirit space.

An emptiness
A space of open reality
A space for God
Question marks for me.
Tears tempered with a pause
In this moment, I am.

And presents stowed
in Santa's sleigh for mailing
Leaves me with great sadness --
And with that, I bid good night.

Ancient Fissures Run Deep

Somewhere, deep down, away and gone
Pain and grief move at subterranean levels
Inertia confounded, gravity defied
Tertiary movements, unheralded moments
signify voids incomparable
Loss once inconceivable.
    Dissipating seminal moments
Longing for a satiation
    That corrupted with ghostly placentas
Prayers uttered, now empty
    Now answered
        Another day when God's "Yes," was "No."
        And the sweetness of contemplation
Turned to the vinegar of
    hoped for peace, not Naomi's *mara*.
No desire for bitterness here --
    A blessed relief
    a blessed release
Where head and heart
Not yet in sync
Invoke an arithmetics of difference
    Thank you Audre Lorde
    For that mathematical phrase
    Which sums up
   my awareness of now.

Ancient Fissures Run Deep

A call to aid and abet
My pain and that of others
the envy of now
Not really, simply un-actualized
Un-activated grief
In the chrysalis stage
Emerging, breaking through
Bubbling forth
As envy
Died within
Years before
It could be born.

(Ancient Fissures continued)

I want not
your joys
And accomplishments
Else I must embrace your sorrows
Your grieves, your pains and doubts
Your cataclysmic, phenomenal angst
Buried so deeply within
That any fissures that signal
An opening, are quickly filled in
Glazed over with a façade of
Dysfunctionality that lets one
function without killing the psyche
The harm done – measured
Death dealing rancor, until
the day
Enough is enough
And a spiritual breakthrough
Of epic proportions
Engorges one's reality
Heart, mind, body, soul
When on must --
Cannot help but
Vomit, expel those encumbrances
Separating true self from true self
And another side of self was born.

Not a new self of two flesh
a new oneness of self-articulating through
the regurgitation of forgotten pain
As a new, fragile
Genuine self, teeters
On the brink of new discoveries
A new dance
For God and I.

And breathing
From a different space
Renewed in present time
Humbled by the majestic
Bitter sweetness of it all

Thinking, feeling
Breathing spent
A new sense of quiet
Ascends
And for now
That's enough.

Let it be
For that's all there is
That's all that need be.
For when things fall a part
or seem to fall apart
Sometimes
They actually come together.

For Mothers Who Desire

For mothers who wanted swollen tummies
And full wombs and sweet potato toes
And your bodies
or life didn't deliver
an infant, a child
a likeness of you
We honor your pain
That deep primordial grief
Permeating your DNA.

Holding you in your grief
The questions remaining unanswered
"Why not, God?"
"How come she had eight,
and we could produce none?"
"How could you allow a Susan Smith
two sweet, sweet boys
She delivered into a watery grave?"
"How could you allow
a woman deranged
To cast three innocent, beautiful lives
Into the cold, murky waters of
San Francisco Bay?"

What manner of evil is this?
What do we do
when we experience betrayal
of and from our bodies;
of and from the power, the God we love?
How could God say "No!"
To one devoted to God
to one committed to love of God, self, neighbor;
to one with such deep desire
to procreate, to parent, to care?

And your answer, God, was "No!"
And your answer was/is long after the fact.

Only when one is ready to hear
When a level of awareness is --
Is one able to hear,
and You reveal:
Her path is different
Her path is to love in other ways
To be there **for the Dad** who also had desires
to be a vessel
to speak for those who cannot speak their pain.
Such is their pregnancy
Her pregnancies.

And for others who wanted to mother
And their bodies produced not
And adoption failed to be an option
Find safe ways
To deal with your grief
Know the betrayal, the butterfly
Embrace the sadness
Scream at God
Be in the moment
Let go of regrets
Fully experiencing these
Emotional aftershocks
In moments, months, years
If needed
Ultimately affords a release
that stuffing feelings
Can never appease.
And one day,
The grieving is not so heavy
The ache no longer so deep
The disappointment not as caustic.

The what-ifs disparate
The regrets tucked away
And peace no longer takes
 a holiday
And compassion for self, abounds
Wrapped in love's sweetness
Blanketed by hope
Now the butterfly
We soar.

Fear Visits

Fear, grips my heart
Like a vise
Holding so tightly –
Suffocating . . . .
My joy, my health.

Fear of what?
Not sure.
Mortality? His, perhaps, not mine.
Of debt? YES!!!!

Quaking, when bills come in

Never sure of how much –
To whom? For what?
Not judgment, not ridicule;
Not reprimand:
Just integrity.

With integrity, one spends responsibly
Can spend with joy and anticipation
Fear is not, and need not be present.

With lack of integrity
Comes humiliation, dread,
Shame, disappointment:
Great pain.

As the inability to pay
Can become personal,
debt beyond my capacity
Is loathing to my sensibility

Makes me nauseous
Grips my heart.

And now having purged this fear for now,
I release and move on.

Opportunity

Sadness lurked around her heart
And grasped, felt, tampered with her mind
Yet the dawn of a new day
and her task was to be.
Be in the moment.
"Be not dismayed!" She knew God would take care of her today,
She knew she could not fret about yesterday;
Yesterday was, and "quote the Raven, nevermore."

        She hadn't wanted to not have finished
        These tasks, so close to the holidays
        and when thinking and focused,
        Recognized each day is a **holy** day
        Holy days are moments
        Opportunities for joy, praise
        For being gentle with herself;
        for limited, for no critique
        About life
        About herself.

Opportunity

She needed to be her own friend--
And if she embraced the sadness,
and let go of being angry with herself,
Then she could smell roses.
For not having met her own expectations
In bloom or not;
See butterflies
Could breathe ever so gently
in the now
And breathing, a gift of life
not all can ever take for granted
Keeps her in gratitude--
allowed her to know,
 and release the anger.

                    And now what is, is
                    What is left --
                      is opportunity.

And Tears

And tears
animated, just below the surface
Heart beating, palpitations
a dance of intriguing proportions
These gems of celestial moments
Could start as a tinkle
And then puddles, growing, growing
Building to overflowing.

        And tears,
        Feel like tsunamis waiting to be born
        Bearing the weight
        of expectations, tinged with hope
        Framed by disappointment.

                And tears
                that in this moment
                Have no need to fall
                When I remembered to breath
                And to pray, and to let go
                And God said, A-men.

Sister, No Friend

And I didn't take IT out on other folk
This morning
    As the restlessness
        Crept out from its hiding place
    This sister, no friend
        of yours or mine
    Inviting worry
        Pressing me to wear
A cloak of uncomfortableness
with existential angst
that has no bearing
    on reality in this moment
        Unless I become willful:
I want not to flaunt my need to control
That which is not mine to control.

And then a true friend asked
"What can I do for you today?"
    And with that beautiful gesture
God stepped up to the plate and said, "I got this!"
And relief washed over me.

And so?
Is it fear that clutched at a breath
   amidst a task
     that caused me to pause and think
Beyond the mundane and the
        immediate creative notions of the moment?
While fear may instead be
false evidence appearing Real
it remains an energy, of sorts
    Compelling, yes
    Expedient, no
    More like troublesome, invasive, too eager?

Uncertainty

Uncertainty kissed my thoughts upon
Waking this morn, and prayer
and gratitude quickly wiped away
The smudges of doubt
And the day
Framed with love
and acceptance and
letting go was a fleeting
Chorus of hours of praise, and joy and sharing
and music making
From across the miles.

Love ebbed and flowed
Like mighty ocean tides
and now as I take my rest
Uncertainty attempts to penetrate
My will, contentment, and peace --
For it's a feeling, not a fact,
I press prayerfully into
      a good night's sleep.
Having recorded facts and feelings
for fleeting moments in time --
Blessed be.

Sadness

Leaving the group
where laughter rang out
Above quiet murmurs and handshakes
and smiles, some disquiet
A cloak or sadness draped across my shoulders.

And without regret
I acknowledged my visitor
Wondered about its source
Served up several hypothesis
Not quite sure of its origins
Sighed, and it passed
Resignation hemmed and hawed
Recognition registered fatigue
Knowing fatigue, anger, hunger, and confusion
Fuels wants.

To rest I went;
To God I released --
The need to know and understand
Leaves empty a space
To be filled with gratitude.

Pensive Moments

Hours after dawn
When brain waves go a flutter
When "what if's" probably run on
Collision courses of 'how comes'
an engagement of mind, body, spirit
Championing the
sacred fonts of endorphins
Touching the outer reaches of God
Brought blurred images,
frayed memories and
Convulsed emotions into
Focused gratitude.

And whispered prayers of thanksgiving
Afforded an awareness of that moment
and this moment and the now
Laughing at "the 12th of Never"
Laughing at the self
whose ego, for a twinkling moment or two
Forgets that Spirit connection
And the One in charge
the One who loves, unconditionally
the One who created and said
Creation was good.

And as day, became night;
Little instances of discovery--

Intimacy shared
Empathy given
a disappointment here and there
All experienced
Then consumed,
And gone.
For the now, ever present God
Walked with and carried us today.

And so we rest
Knowing day is done – The day was, we are --
The morrow we greet
When it becomes today,
Launched with no regrets.

Exuberant Resignation

The instant
Recognition of peace
Engulfs one's soul.
One is content, resigned
to one's life
Of change and sameness
Of grace and chaos,
of joy and sorrow and in between.

For decades--much joy, many accomplishments
Had framed sensibilities
Rooted in love, integrity, and respect
Echoes of blessing.

Illusive Answers

Topsy turvy--
What is, becomes what was;
Answers that were definitive
Become answers no more, or maybes
Uncertainty lurks back into the present.
Things hoped for
towards completion of--
In this moment are in limbo
And now, waiting, trusting,
Letting go, letting God.
A mantra for all things
Mysterious, half understood
incomplete, unfinished, left behind.

Restlessness

Wispy fleeting thoughts
Like organdy
    the kind that's not yet starched
Mirroring gossamer wings of angels
Cloaking the mysterious
saluting the moment
    shaky, fragility of uncertainty;
requiring a strength
Born of a power
Transcendent of humanity;
Desperately needed by us
in moments of vulnerability
Sensing rapid heart rate
And shallow breathing--
Acknowledgement of restlessness.

And, that restlessness
Opens a door, many doors--
Doors of our own choosing,
Leading to chambers of creativity or self-pity
To anticipating liberation or calculated dread
To an immediacy
Not quieted by thoughts.

Anguished Indignation

Contempt is not the space of this moment;
Frustration is.
Lack of integrity and callous disregard
Work to irritate my serenity, the peace worn
during a time of year when
Aromas of frenzy and trauma drama
Permeate our atmosphere
Sitting with inner turmoil.

In response to another's misbehavior:
an inability to make good choices
Tests my capacity to let go and let God.
And what is my part I all of this?
Knowing in this moment
A sickness, dread, a hopelessness.

Visions

Purge self of anything antithetical
to God-framed life
Clear away clutter
Clean up relationship with self:
Best possible self-care.

Tumultuous Joy

Glorious instances of overwhelming ecstasy
Pulsates within
As divine witness permeates all my being
A call to prophetic engagement
A birth, rejuvenation, transference
   sanctification of holiness.
Within and without
a declaration to embrace fully
Divine grace changing your soul
From time immemorial
to present moments made sacred
By the profound God presence
The unmitigated enveloping of a new reality
Shifting perspectives
Transforming old pain healed mightily
to new perspectives and insights
On the is-ness of this life
World without end.

Before and since the foundation of the world
And taking on a new mantle of ministry
New heights set forth before God
So it is, so let it be done.

All Desire for God

Awesome, magnificent power
Touches us with each breath
Each inhale made holy.

At Rest

Gliding above a sea of purple cotton,
Gigantic, plush carpet
Suspended in air just below
As oft in the distance
Southeast as the crow flies
Waves of red heather frames
 the sky's gossamer flooring.

Red fades to orange to orange red to pink
As dawn breaks and little girls and moms
and dads and grown men, and boys and families
sleep as we sail cross country
on God's wings and nuns' prayers.

Gently we come into the morning
In praise, in thanksgiving
that God allowed someone the intellect
the creativity to defy gravity
And like birds we soar above ground in flight.

Having appreciated creation
Desire to rest for but a while
as adventure greets the day
And now, what was pink
Has become soft tangerine --
The carpet thick, indented --

At Rest

A deep gorge, not a valley in
    the shadow of death
but seas of life --
A birth-day
A new day
And now yellow fades away.

The sun once hinting existence
breaks through in divine glory
And purple fleece transmogrified
Now acres of thick, intertwined rope:
fused, forms curtains to stave off
that radiance below
And then the looping, tangled rope
shifts to fuzzy, gossamer triangles
some with sharp angles,
other wisps of threads.

Some whirls of taffeta
and now descending through
more sparks of tulle than will ever
be used anywhere in weddings this year.

And descending again
Into layers of nothingness
that shields us from that radiance--
And the earth sleeps
For brown surrounds itself,
in more brown
of winter.

Seasons

Fatigue, exhaustion drifted across
the country as you said good morning --
Knowing your illness is --
Knowing that in the scheme of things
a repertoire of personal and communal prayer
Is/was the response.

How vulnerable you must feel--
How fragile our lives together
How devastating these changes
as vulnerability frames our reality together
And so I cry tears of acceptance as
I can't, God can, and Words of
"Lord have mercy," permeate my heart space
Reaching out and touching others
Prop up my sagging spirits,
Seeking more information
made clear there is more to do

And you have not given up--
In dialogue God says, not yet.

Breathing and letting go.
I sigh and give thanks
When a sister-friend phones
Her voice, her prayers reach out, touch me
Hold, embrace, bolster, encourage.

And it is that moments turn
to hours and you feel better;
And it is in trusting God, loving self,
that calm surrounds me;
comes over me.

For only this day, will I, can I
be present, for this day --
in faith and hope
for healing.

And in the moment, the buoyant
Joy of yesterday, becomes a new joy
which accompanies me, this day
The sun has begun to set in the West
A yellowish tint dances north
in the atmosphere
As rapidly comes the close of day.

Joy Takes Delight

Joy, sparkling, rejuvenating
sanctified holy unspeakable ecstasy
charges my soul, so powerfully
that I soar and dance as I walk
Radiate powerfully as I talk
Such comfort and peace
 undeniably incredible.

Such satisfied inspiration, incalculable
As the ancient of days anoints the moment
charging each nanosecond with
gifted realities of possibilities;
Now, right now this moment
Not then, not tomorrow, but now
When now, the immediacy of this moment
slips back into past or forward into future;
 now disappears
God connection disappears
And make-pretend worship
　　　becomes idolatry.

Joy, sweet joy, joy indefinable
Joy, powerful, compassionate
Joy, dynamic, warmth
Joy: divine glory, hallelujah, Rejoice!

Joy Takes Delight

Joy ecstatic touch moving
soul/spirit, mind, body
Divine movement: joy --
And the joy; joy, sacred, sacred joy
fa ith, hope, love—incarnated joy:

Joy: anointing of God: joy
Joy: the space and place of grace and mercy
Joy: Delight in God with us now;
Joy: Honoring Imago Dei with our DNA
Joy: restlessness made calm
Joy: doubt transferred into hope
Joy: jubilant life as gift. Joy.
Above mountains below valleys
Traversing oceans, seas, rivers, streams.
Joy: in the elegance of a butterfly
Joy: majesty of a waterfall
beauty of sunrise and sunset
Joy: power of great lions and tigers
Joy: memory of an elephant
Non-circumstantial existence
Joy: love and grace supreme.

Complexity of Breathing

To live is to breathe;
To breathe is to live.
Without breathing, one cannot live.
The gift of moving air through our bodies
      effortlessly –
           Too many take for granted,
must not be taken lightly,
undermined or assumed:
Patients of emphysema, lung cancer,
asthma, know not the capacity to . . . . just breathe.

Disappointment

Makes you wanna holler –
The craziness of bad decision making
Justified, impulse spending
Rattling your peace, challenging your joy
Getting sick and tired of being sick and tired,
about old problems.

Knowing that doing the same thing
and expecting different results is idiotic--
How can love and sanity be so conflicted,
Reason and logic so blurred, defined, ignored
Missing in action?

Does illness or disease
    trump best practices?
Where does compassion and empathy
   begin and end and responsibility emerge?
What does it mean to let go and let God?
 Is God too busy to show up and show out?
The poets say: God never fails;
    God has promised to never
leave or forsake us.

Belief is supreme in the concept
    the inner voice connects and beliefs
Holds on to trust
   framed by a reality that presses
and prods and seeks to intimate,
    Discourage, make crazy
The gift of trust –

For when lies and truth cannot
be acknowledged, cannot
be reconciled even when
framed by disease, by addiction--
A need for immediacy of
   Let go, Let God
Presses so dearly, so nearly
   Believe, surrender, and acceptance
Are the only options.

That is, surrender and experiencing serenity
Or drown in the what if's,
the pain of disappointment and betrayal,
Only with surrender
Is there room for God to be in charge.

Whispered prayers

In words and feelings
    with pink flamingos
On hard hospital chairs
    Amid the wings of birds
We pray; God responds --
    Signifying with grand majesty
Compassion soaring
    God speaks symphonically
Empathy declaring
    "I love you!"
My desire is not for you to suffer
    My dream for you is to embody love
To grow, to be in community.

For prayers do change things
As such, sound frames our needs
    Beyond our wildest imagination
    Beyond our ability to think
the holiness of now
When God whispered
We listened
A prayer became real.

Waiting

In the mystery of life's moments
When "in sickness and in health"
    Become really, real
A God consciousness, is even
more important, that we may be at
peace when crisis explodes
about us, when others must help;
    and we must be empathetic for they
move slower than we'd like
when those we love are ill.

And so we prayerfully wait
We ask for what is needed
We inquire, we persist as
someone we love is not well.

We press again and again
    for they depend on us
We sit vigil, prayerful
    With content; we pause
and give thanks.

Exercises in Serenity

As empty trolleys rumble past
   open hospital room doors
      As patients sleep, some with restlessness

Gentle snoring, sometimes moaning
     as pain accompanies their journey
        of hopeful healing
    with much struggle, much effort
And wheelchairs, walkers
    the step, step, slide, slide of feet
       In rehab, in hope.

Bodies cut, opened, prodded, massaged
    reshaped, re-sectioned, sown, sutured, stapled together --
      Bodies repaired, touched by angels
        As prayers trickle down, move about
          spread abroad on behalf of
      the sick, the wounded, the healing
    the dying, those cured, those while healed
  are not cured,
and soon take their eternal rest.

And we breathe, and we – family, friends,
   lovers, spouses, children honor our
     God-given lives, celebrating love
        With each breath, each heartbeat,
     each experience of laughter
   in gratitude
For even when we shall breathe no more
     When someone calls our name
       we are here.
        When we touch someone's life
     the memories permeate the universe
And exist forever.

Full Moons

Move with authority
through the heavens
As our feelings about life,
about ourselves wax and wane;
Ebb and flow over the vicissitudes
that move about within
our psyches our spirits, our bodies
As we attempt to
Control, cajole, create, cause, cure
That which we never could.
Fashion, fix, frame
For life itself – at times
More tenable – true createdness
more terrifying – as vulnerable reality
more free – as electrifying space
Charged with making us whole, again.

Fires Among us

What was a growing fire
With volcanic embers
Spewing forth trivia and the mundane --
Deep desire for peace
flanked by
Deeper desire to control, fix
Remove, eradicate pain;
Turn back the clock
Reorient reality.

Those fires are less than smoldering embers
For I looked to God
Opened so God could touch me
Resumed the responder of "I Am"
Who brought more laughter
and love into my life
As the last spark, petered out.

A Celebrated Life

A beautiful elegance in motion
where your love so radiates,
that others see, feel, sense
the splendor of it all
Wrapped in the warmth of
silent embraces.

As you speak of your beloved
And your beloved speaks of you
One celebrates the breath of
their lover breathed three weeks ago
One completing the other's sentences;
Hearts beating synchronously,
Reveling in the accomplishments of the other
Praising and thanking God
For two hearts meeting;
Beating, conducting
Symphonic layers of love:
Unconditional,
Inexplicable,
Magnanimous,
Magnificent,
Of God.

Goodnight Sun

As sun sets
And day fades into night
As celestial choir, starry with fame and romance
prepare to dance and
twinkle across the heavens;
We give thanks and salute the one who
draws back the curtains across time
And lowers them at eventide.

We rejoice and give thanks
That for today
Notions of nevermore have been
silenced among us; replaced by life vitality
Beating hearts gathering in community
Together shouts accolades of Hallelujah!

Divine Seduction

And when God kissed
Created order
Bringing dawn to a new day
Appropriate response was/is
to fall prostrate in joy, humility, and gratitude
Greeting Beloved Almighty with
our whole selves, unabashedly
in awe and expectation.

An Incredible Light

Something amazing happened:
I saw you, you reflected God, back to me,
Reminding me that something amazing
happens each day.
Beyond circumstances and the 101 stuff of life that
often is not my business anyway:
    Amazing: God
    Amazing: Life with God
    Amazing: God and you and me
    Amazing: God's phenomenal creations
    Amazing: To taste, touch, see, smell
    The incredible, glory of God!

Mystical Moments of Joy

In greeting others
Mystical moments of joy burst forth
As spirits connect with spirit,
As mind engages powerfully
In only that instance when
God consciousness embraces,
explodes, radiates, in and around and between
Connecting hearts
Aware of, not dependent upon
Packaging, framing, status – acquired or perceived.

For in the seconds of encounter
    Framed, fueled, and founded in God
Circumstances, nor powers, nor principalities
    Can ultimately rob the connection of Grace;
Grace embodied and personified is love.

Right with God

Powerlessness produces empowerment
Sometimes life seems paradoxical.
What is, seems to be totally opposite
OF what we do; that is, we do
what God calls us to do.
What is simple is not necessarily easy
This day, desire for God is the righteous move.

Oh, to admit powerlessness
is not about victimage or defeat or giving up.
Admitting powerlessness
Engages opportunity, framed, held by
Divine presence, revealed glory.

Doxa (glory): powerful, empowering
Grace: concretized glory
Magnificent love is what is;
Is the possibility to be present
To know the gift of forgiving
 self for shortcomings of yesterday;
To keep breathing, inhaling Spirit
moment by moment in the now;
to resist the need to move too quickly,
forward with plans
Avoiding obsessing about what is right for tomorrow
Weeks away;
while needing to plan some events
that must occur for safety and order
for a morrow, in the not too distant future.
God grant me the serenity this day:
To accept the unchangeable
To change the changeable
To discern differences between can and cannot.
Spirit breathe in me today
moment by moment
as **everything** is surrendered unto You.

Riding the Seas

What happens when
reality, rife with chaos, pain, discomfort
And one is in and not of it;
as we ride the waves of the seas of life
Sometimes sitting quietly, resting in
the bow of the ship
with God as Captain and crew;
When seas and waters of rivers
are calm, and when seas and rivers, even oceans
are contentious and turbulent--
Whatever the state of those waters
Of the waters of life.

We are not the storm, or the wave in the sea
We are passengers
on a journey betwixt birth and death
With joy and pain and happiness and sadness
All coming upon us, as the Spirit
Desires to bring love, comfort, wholeness
Yet the angst, craziness, the teeming
random, cacophonic juxtapositions
of sanity and peace combating.

Slapped Back to Faith

When dawn arose this day
and she knew he didn't know her name
At least, he couldn't tell her his name
and it seemed he didn't know her
Though later he said his name--
Parts of her foundation rocked.

She shaved him
as he rambled on with a litany
of words of fighting and oppression
Not words of encouragement, as days before --
Not words about weather, family, faith,
politics, health, life, hope;
The words were repetitive
She knew not whether any part of him
that spiritual, mental part of him
Connected with her—

Knew not if he was speaking metaphorically
If one of those syllabus reflected materials
recently thought, or beliefs or ideas
something long forgotten;
the ramblings of a brilliant mind
that at that moment was not present to anyone.

She sighed, she pray, she cried;
She cried some more.
Never had she felt this total, massive depth
of vulnerability, helplessness, anxiousness, fear.
She recognized the complexity of the
human mind, body, soul;
She knew the fleetingness of sanity
One instant, one medication, one seeming, random act
The switch that doesn't get through
Synapses charging, misfiring.

Another Day

On the morning of the fourth day
As dawn has broken,
And the day marches toward noon
I sigh, pray, contemplate
Not the day, but this moment
Changed with responsibilities
as you lay listless, quiet
I pray you know angels are watching over you.
And then he woke up.

Restless Gratitude, Formidable Challenges

In the moment, in worship
As folk meet and greet
as we waited to proclaim
Our spirit brood like a hen waiting for her chicks
Waiting for them to reassemble with order,
So we can move toward the reason we are here.

Time presses on--
self must be still, ego silent
As we yoke our restlessness
In gratitude: all challenges
Fall away
As we focus on God, and God alone.

Listen to Me

Talking my head off
Telling you he's hurting
Day in and day out
When crises comes
And I get all in your face
because when I communicated
You failed to listen
And now you try to placate me
with excuses and platitudes
Of "no problem," when there is a problem
And I need you to hear me
Get the urgency of the moment
Take responsibility
And step up to the plate.

        Handle the situation
        Before things get worse
        and the next time someone speaks
        Do us all a favor:
        Listen attentively for the problem
        If you don't have the answers
        Then find someone who does.

                Explain the possibilities of what's going on
                Explain to the patient their responsibilities
                in the care
                And do the righteous thing
                By being forthcoming

Doing preventative work
And not waiting until it escalates
And becomes a problem
Before you act!

Gift of Grief and Shame

When I think of a gift
that intelligence, hard work,
and even God's grace may not afford me in life,
I know grief and shame.

Poignant Dissonance

Grief struck a chord today
The dissonance:
Eerie, sharp, poignant --
A pain the taste of bitterest herbs
Warping tastes of anything sweet
amid the cornucopia
of Life's essential goodness.

As Ecclesiastes people --
We experience many seasons of life:
Time to be born,
Time to die;
Time to give;
Time to receive.
Time to give;
Time to take.
Time to control;
Time to let go of control.
Time to feast;
Time to fast.
Time to laugh;
Time to cry.
Time to work;
Time to rest.

When listening totally,
With heart and soul
We appreciate life more fully.

With empathy, love, and courage
We embrace difficult journeys
Not regretting of fretting "What's so."
Not becoming victim or
Ensnared in denial.

Not envious or jealous
For we know not the
true paths or realities of others.

Seeing that which is terminal
That which is dissonant and discordant
As opportunities for
Prayer: dialogue with a power much greater
Position: locating oneself in faith
Possibility: Looking and seeing
    what can happen today.

Mysterious Moments

Thoughts bubble up
Amid feelings that flow wide and deep:
rooted in faith
grants a reprieve
that something, someone
Much greater than I
has the answers
Cares about me
And holds me
as things seem to fall apart.

In those times
of most vulnerability
Awe, ambiguity, and uncertainty,
When anxiety and fear
Crouch about my heels
Like hungry dogs
who bark, yipping, yipping--
They too, only want
Someone to notice them;
to pass them a morsel of food.
Looking down, I smile
See them clearly
in the eyes
Defying the fear
that tickles their noses
as the scents from my body
Queue them of my discontent.

Brought back to this moment
I breathe
saying "No" to the uncomfortable
"Yes," to a seeming
Erosion of certainty.
"Yes," to possibility for rebirth,
renewal, for being grounded in love:
a love so brilliant,
That amid mystery
accords peace.

Sad Puddles

Sorrow dripping from the eaves
of the soulful house
Congealed as frozen tears --
Making puddles
On the carpeted patios of their beings.

Sadness tumbles
Like stars of the milky way
Illuming ghosts, past and future
the fatigue of seeing,
of revelation;
The incarnation of a truth
Tempers this imagination
toward healing.

A Closed Chapter

Pain had seemed to disappear months ago
When she thought
She'd fully let go of
Caring about her barren situation;
that she was over needing
to see a swollen belly
to hear the heartbeat
to glimpse the fragile fetus
on the ultra sound.

She thought those dead dreams
had been laid to rest;
that this blessed experience
was no longer important.
that this chapter had closed
And no such books
ever to be written.
Yet the flicker of light
of weighted need to be pregnant
to carry to term, to nurse,
To diaper, to hold, to nurture, to adopt . . . .
Still causes tears to well up.

And she prays
that these too, will past.
That giving birth
to ideas, books, and projects
Songs, and poems
that mothering from afar to grown folks
Can be enough.

Moments, Motions, Experiences

Motions
Rhythms
Life forces
Mingling, dancing;
whimsical moments
in time and space
Joviality
intertwined above
the Mediocrity
Hypocrisy
shellacked to the
Surfaces of our minds.

Can we see in the moment
beyond facades
shimmering instances
of truth, realities.

Can one be present
and yet be discarded;
be ignored, be spoken
Like one isn't there.

Anger seeks out, my pores
amid my experiences of your
Disingenuousness.
False, fake fronts
with Smiles attached.

You think you know
What's wrong
What's certain
What's real;
I wonder which mirrors
Are you using
For a lens.

Grace & Laughter

Grace & wonder
and joy
Is this an illusion?
Is it really, really real
or a figment of my imagination
Shall we pretend this bliss?
I embrace the issues
of the now
And say, praise God
—And laugh!

Monster Toys

Monsters lurk about,
Come in many forms
Like kiddy toys;
Those jack-in-the-boxes
that just pop up, unexpectedly
When you least expect them:
Surprise! Surprise!
They bounce up, in your face,
and we get thrown for a loop
    We react,
    We hurt, we know anger
    We failed to anticipate
    We forgot to laugh.
    It's just a silly old toy,
    And we took it too seriously.

We forgot the big and the small stuff
Jumps at us all the time
in moments of life
When we're most vulnerable,
When we feel our weakest,
Here comes old jack-in-the-box
    Scaring us silly!
We get scared when we pay attention
To stuff that's not our own;
    We take stuff too seriously,
We fill ourselves with other people's stuff
    and we get sick and feel bad.

So laugh, from your toes
(Don't forget you can laugh that low,
And you don't even have

to cut your toenails to do so!)
    Laugh until your tummy jiggles
    Like soft Jello!

Laugh in the face of threat and betrayal
Take a deep breath
    And leap for joy
    Exposing the culprit
When the Jack-the-the-box
The Jill-on-the-hill
    Comes to upset you
    To rob you of your joy
    Just laugh, laugh, laugh loudly.

Laughter melts the pain
and takes away the sting
Laughter eases tension
and helps us readjust our bodies;
    That the pain cannot
    Turn up the levels of acidity
and toxins in our bodies
To levels that make us sick.

So dance and leap for joy
Run, joy, run.
    Do yoga, qi-gong, tai-chi,
    Tae-bo, shadow boxing
    Tennis, golf, walk;
Name your body prayer
And embrace that prayer
as a practical daily opportunity
To keep yourself well;
To face down the monsters
To live and let live;
If I must hurt,
Let it be from laughter.

Fires Engulfed, Flowing Fresh Waters Heal

Anger, rage, venom,
chokes me so that
I can barely breathe.
Coming to awareness about
What my life has to be like
to meet another's needs:
Like an earthquake and a volcano hit!
I can barely breathe.

Like running hundreds of miles
No--millions and millions of miles
Running away, I suppose
from the truth
That I must contain myself
Not let any buttons get pushed
To deal with this anger
That feels organic
For mutuality is out of the door
On a lot of issues.

I must exercise daily
to flush what needs
to be felt and acknowledged;
Otherwise it spews forth
through my pores

and plays out in many, many ways.
I must write daily,
Stop and flush what needs to be spoken
For words unuttered spew forth in body language.

I need to know that it's OK
To feel what I feel
To think what I think.

It's OK
Otherwise:
I drown in my own pain
I become victim;
I hold off until
I regurgitate.

I feel sad, and disappointed
hurt, perhaps taking things personally:
Brain damage can't be reasoned with.
My self-righteousness
will merely create more pain
as we only have borrowed time.

I must choose each moment
And each moment,
and each moment:
to listen, hear, release, love;
Listen, hear, release, love,
Empathize, laugh,
Creatively deal with all things in life.
Remembering I am not
my life's circumstances.
We are who we are
Life has given us some alum,
One must look toward grace
and flowing fresh waters.

Rage by Noon

Nausea bubbling
Distorting reality,
Betrayal felt
Creeping up, encroaching hot lava
falling from Vesuvius --
"My God, my God,
Why have you forsaken me?"

Grace in *absentia*
offers no comfort, no solutions;
No peace.
My entrails cry out
in ways unfathomed by my mind.
My spirit, in empathy
Wails and moans.
The level of incredulity
pain, and angst overflowing:
a cauldron of acid
Dispels the hope
that everything is OK.

Baptized Rage Unfurled

Fury bubbles up when thinking
about our reality, about another's pain and suffering
One intimate to me, whose breath weeks ago
Warms my being, to this other's pain.
Troubles my spirit and shakes my faith
At its very depths,
My connecting with God this day
Feels wounded, shaken;
filled with angst.

A Belly of Faith

Pain down in her bowels
Afforded a disconnect from her soul's self
Twisted up, locked down
Like botulism
Poisoning every fiber of her being
Wracked with rage of discontent.

        Disappointments trouble her inner calm
        Her divinely-given majestic presence
        in moments of high anxiety
        Easing, slipping, seeping through
        out of, in between viscera
        tiny, itsy, bitsy soul particles
        oozing out from cells, corpuscles.

Dripping into the earth, who wails
and moans and groans for us, for you,
for all who suffer loss.
Earth shutters and wails
and quickens in hurt;
faints with pain.

Dawn Breaks

At the dawn of Day,
as God spoke--
Above my head,
a full moon shimmers.
I know a joy, a gratitude
beyond compare.

Surprises Dance in Splendor

In short order, an invitation
uttered changes, many things
perspectives, dynamics of time
acknowledgement and some delight.
Being tapped to take on new responsibilities
which may mushroom into an
adventure of unknown proportions.

For now I sleep, I rest
before dawn begins a new day.

Guilty Grief

Weighted down by hours, days, years
of grief, of stuff laboring
Amid life's tragic moments--
Not aware of holding on
to events and long dead choices
of things forgivable,
of options lost
Ideas explored and tossed:
of things said;
of things sad.

Holy Bliss: A Kiss of God

Awakened once more by Grace and mercy
Moving about the tasks of the day
Schedules to keep, places to be
on time, moving, greeting, caring for my beloved.
And we moved from our space
to get to the appointed place
and dawn had not quite broken.

Moving out on the street
Our eyes were kissed by God
as we beheld the moon with powerful radiance
a moon full, couched in the heavens
AT once framed by silhouettes of trees
In another instance, ensconced by fleeting clouds.

So powerful, so engaging, so marvelous
Such splendor, such magnificence, such a kiss
Took my breath away--
As such a gift so early in our day
Invoked tremendous gratitude and love and passion
Creating a loving, deep desire
A moment of intimacy
Between God and me
Oh, joy unspeakable.

Crashed and Burned

Restlessness jiggled her sensibilities
As she looked to focus on the day;
Sluggishness and agitation
Dropped themselves over her shoulders
Dissatisfaction covered her feet
Before she could dash out the door to meet the day.

      An old friend of Perfectionism
      and close cousin Must Control
      Visited before she could get another prayer through
      and then she prayed,
      and reached out to share
      With a friend who would understand.

And realized she was coming
out of an emotional hangover
from the stuff of yesterday
and then she let go and let God
and got in the day
Knowing the importance of
being gentle with herself
and letting God take charge
    And take care of her,
    and everybody else today.

A Holiday from Acceptance

Agitation trickled through her veins
Disquieting moments
    pricked her consciousness
As an internal dialogue
a skirmish played itself out
as she wondered why her spirit
seemed restless, mind unfocused,
body lethargic
Realizing she was stuck in the "what ifs"
    the hour comes and
    why nots and used to's
Was removing her from God's presence,
mercy and grace.
And so she prayed to be in the moment
To accept life as life is today
    to release yesterday and
    to stand in the now of this hour
Knowing it's OK to be
with her agitations and disquiet
For when she inhaled the Holy Spirit
And exhaled, releasing anything contrary
    to this anointing power
    She then moved toward
being comfortable in her skin that day.

Staying close to God
Being God focused, daily
    moment by moment by nanosecond
    is always her prime directive
And is especially essential
    on days
        when it feels
She's not on the top of her game.

When her praise is present
    yet hidden,
Gratitude in place, yet muted,
      Confession clears
Emotional, spiritual, mental clutter
    And then she comes
To her true self
The one God makes this day
    And then, Joy quietly,
        slowly, peacefully
            Comes again.

From the Brink of a Breaking Point:
This Too, will Pass

(i)

Almost strangled by life's vicissitudes--
stress, pain, fatigue, and weary thoughts--
Trapped someplace between the now,
the then, the tragedy, the comedy,
Music rescued him.
Renewed his faith; helped him
reconnect with his authentic self
Reminded him of the faithfulness of God
reiterated to him that . . . this too, will pass.

(ii)

Having not met his own needs
Having been disconnected
Having dampened down, ignored
        his sensual, sexual self
Having been smothered in the
        details of day in and day out
Melt down, brought him
back together as a unified self
To acknowledge the
Fragility of time of him of them
. . . this too, will pass.

(iii)

Aware . . . . this too, will pass
Aware of his tattered, beautiful,
fractured, fragile,
    full-of-life amazing self

he breathes, therefore he is
his soul ruminates
his body capitulates
his mind cogitates
his ego sleeps
his authentic self rejoices
as "this too will pass"
Ceases to rule him today.

An Obituary for the Never born

Excitement, no ecstasy permeated our thoughts
Our being, our lives
We were pregnant, a baby was coming to our home --
No wonder I'd fall asleep at my desk;
No wonder my clothes didn't fit;
No wonder fishy smells made me sick,
    even in clean spaces;
And a few hours and a blood test later
And we had news of rejoicing
And we told everyone.

And a week later,
in the time it took God to make a world
that which was,
ceased to be
Nevermore.

Fleeting Furies

Awareness electrifies the moment
when awakening a tone of thoughts
Drown in the instances of being, of thought
Want to ruminate across the day
Just at the break of dawn –

And sighing, prayers lift upward
Seeking to quiet the storms of angst,
of disquiet, bordering on seeds of resentment.

Not wanting that path
Seeking place
Breaking solitude, reaches out to another
whose wisdom exceeds and encourages
and whose compassion spreads
like warm butter over toast--
And, awareness becomes an
opportunity not opposition
To serenity, deeply desired.

And knowledge of awareness
says it's OK to be where we are;
And more prayers can beckon God
to help this all make sense,
as extending trust to God
opens doors windows, and gates of heaven
towards accepting current realities
Serving as catalyst
for appropriate action.

And just knowing insanity is --
And sanity emerges
Moves one back into today
not overwhelmed and stuck in
the past, that did not unfold;
not stressed over the future
The particulars which remain hidden
In the hush of the moment
In the synchronicity of mindfulness--
An airplane just flew over.

Galvanized Grief, Gangrenous Guilt

Choked by thoughts and feelings
of regrets and losses
Exacerbates and expands the grief
of what could have been-
How deep the angst
How visceral the pain
      which leapt up from beneath
      those bowels so ladened
      with guilt as to become cement.

Thwarted when grasping for hope
Daunted when holding to faith
The weight of it all so overwhelming:
a need for purging, for release,
for acceptance and self-forgiveness
rippled through the atmosphere.

Deep longing for sweet peace and serenity
Became a pressing desire
A quest of that moment, begun
with awareness, found the import
of surrender.

Surrender to what is
The moment, an increment
of divine love and wisdom;
Each moment embraced --
chips away at the debt,
the depth of guilt.

Allows an experience of grief
as present moments are more than
the norm, than the exception.
Pain dissipates
as Fall moves to Winter, to Spring, and Summer
Moments in the days of one's life
Afford more joy amid the mourning;
Little flickers of hope emerge
every once and a while.

Revelation, Release, Regroup, Restore

When grief has waited/weighted
You down amongst the oscillations of life--
When anger has shut you down
and your rage bubbles over,
cancerous in its movement
making pathological everything
in its midst –

When relationships turn upside
down and it feels like all is wrong;
all against you
when you can't get your hair right
And weight fluctuates
and you're not loving on
your own self; well--
The time is to wait on, and rest in God.

Resting in God
slows us down,
so we can
hear and know
    Divine comfort.

Wisp of Frustrated Reality

Rocking in motion
Going, running, uncentered, not connectivity
Leaves one woefully
Unstable, not God focused
like a runaway train.
Terror instills,
no one has safety
as the spirit falters
    For fear, dried up in our bones
    Implodes on us.

And we are left
   spiritually emaciated
     in jail, outside
         privy, not to ourselves, or others,
           Locked away in fantasies
                That were never to be;
         were not of God for us
       as the ego run riot
    Causes unnecessary pain
   But God cares, intimately
to care, to love.

A Volcanic Moment

Saw, no felt a moment
of something bubbling beneath
the surface – acidic, like lava
Mt. Vesuvius redux within
something tamped down within
Like lava – hot smoldering
Needing to explode
And for an instant, or two, or three.

Awareness of those energies
presented themselves
in such furor
I was almost taken aback
That such rage
Lingered within.

Vulnerability

Cacophony of pain
Compresses one's cranium
Permeates the reality of now
Trying to speak louder than God
Moving one's body, doing body prayers
and uttering verbal prayer to override
the narcissism of negativity.

    Alphabet soup of angst
    Gumbo of desire for peace
    Casserole of too many yesterday's
    Thinking and
    Curiosities about tomorrows
    ultimately desires that
    all pain, doubt, fears flee.

        Unbroken record
        Like a gerbil hustling, moving,
        going nowhere fast
        Stuff, cluttering the space
        Belonging uniquely, unequivocally to God;
        I surrender now to this power, to this place
        that offers now, to this power
        to this place
        that opens love,
        Comfort and protection unspoken.

Busted

Busted, bloated, blessed
in meditation, God reminded me
Mind, body, spirit all one
Busted on notions that any
one part of us rocks and rules

Our realities are like a
symphony:
Life is an orchestral work
needing winds, brass, percussion, and strings
Bloated from lack of sleep
and from fatigue and misery
Blessed to know God
and to be mindful about prayers
and work and spiritual growth
Blessed to know change as gift.

Serenity

Missing in action
Feels like the theme of this moment
Feels like the city of Lost
in the county of Frustration
On the street of Exhaustion
in the country of Struggle.
Disappointment and incredulity
Having lost the gift of serenity
In those moments when
Feelings have overrun the
boundaries of balance
and contentment--
Nerves are frazzled;
sleepy, sitting in a meeting.

Working in a foggy
Constellation of gratitude and serenity
Holding fast to this moment
wanting to be a blessing
wanting to be blessed;
Needing to be serene and forward
Not harboring regrets or
embarrassment over things past--
Acceptance: life as is
An openness for possibility
Love: action embracing God
Joy: effervescence
Hope: possibility
Fear: forever engaging all righteousness
Faith: fabulous awareness intentionally thankful, heartfelt.

Circumstances

This day, the second day
Shaped by God, with a day of thanksgiving
that even in your altered state
you proclaimed; I moved forward
Slapped back to faith; my faith;
the faith of family, friends; of our ancestors:

> Those who stayed the course
> believe God kept them
> believe God is keeping you.
> For in whatever place we find ourselves
> Whenever, wherever, wherever--
> We are not our circumstances.

Regardless of our awareness,
God always knows us intimately.
Nothing can separate us from or replace
or rise above or beyond
God's call on our lives
God's compassion, care, concerns for us.
My beloved, this medical crisis
has slapped us back to faith.

A Hot Summer's Day

A moment in a day in a life
at once starts with gratitude
And then wisps of the interjection
of other folks stuff
Sniffing around
Colliding with, collaborating with my
Stuff that can roll over into insanity.

Tickled by annoyance and getting on my
last sanctified nerve, fueled
by a "how dare you"
Kissed ever so gently by
tiny bits of anger, that could be tempted
Be aggravated to transmogrify.

Into all outrage,
Yet swallowing prayer
and the gift of choice, of choosing
Reminds me of who I am, whose I am
who other folks are, and I get it --
I don't have to go to a tempestuous mountain
or a valley of despair
in remembering whose I am –

I cuss ever so softly
In plain English to myself
I get back in my groove--
Hit reset
And smile
And write.

Completion of what could have
been a finale--
Now a moment of acceptance
Knowing this too, will pass.
And in the is-ness of this moment
God is, I am, I am loved;
I can love, I do love,
And all is well.

Trust

Control inhibits trust
Says I know all the answers:
My way is the highway
is hard to navigate--
    If I release
        Then "Let go and Let God,"
           Is more than an adage or clever saying.

Spirituality is simple
Tho' tedious, perhaps difficult,
Yet not impossible.
Given my awareness that
   Control dances around
   my sensibilities, my palette
of colors and ways of being
this privilege provides opportunities
   for growth, heightened
   awareness, release, freedom, peace –
Peace so mysterious
feeling illogical amidst
challenges, conflicts, problems
that can sometimes seem
overwhelming, tough, hard.

And yet, when in the moment
Not in yesterday or tomorrow,
Breathing, tasting God
   Draping the cloak of divine trust
   around shoulders
Became tightened, weighted, tense,
Relaxed, stress free
   When relying on God
    For everything;
Is when
doing so can
shake loose the
weight of the world.

On a Collision Course with Myself

Agitation ruffled the quietness of myself,
The self I woke up with.
    what was the catalyst for this discontent?
    The usual suspects not surfacing
Remembering the wise words of a woman I respect,
sent me to the keyboard
to tickle the ivories as they say--
and I played the hymns of my childhood.

And the music moved me, touched me
that had been dormant for many sunrises
and then as the lava bubbled up inside;
Recognizing I was angry at myself
that I'd somehow let the business of life
and other commitments shut out
The need to sing, to play,
To cloak myself, express myself in sound.

And so, a surprising A-hah moment
that makes my heart beat so quickly
As this realization both saddens me
and intrigues me, as my recent focus
have been at the behest of my call.

And God promised the careers would be parallel;
And it feels impossible to juggle it all;
And then I get the truth, I can't;
That I have to be open to God and the universe
To reveal how to do both
without fear or expectation.

I feel the movement of change within--
a rebirth, like a butterfly wrestling, struggling
to break through the chrysalis.
The good news is I've had the revelation;
with this awareness,
I accept the adventure, and stand
Between the now and the not yet.
For today, I sit with the revealed reality.

Sweet Surrender

Ah, gratitude
For each breath, the gift to see, hear, touch, taste, smell
The blessing of running, jumping, smiling,
The joy of creativity,
Of loving and being love
Of salvific joy,
Freedom to not be controlled or manipulated
By powers and principalities
As Grace brought me into this world
And holds me daily
and empowers and loves me.
    Blessed be,
      as a surrendered soul rejoices.

And Baptized rage,
    Is rage released, rage without power over
    Is rage creatively channeled
Transformed,
Having experienced much grief
and pain, and disappointment
    Realizing some pain
    Emerges from expectations and assumptions
    and having come to such realization
Breathing comes easier
Joy replaces anger
    Grief expended shifts from mourning
    to a place of stillness, of quiet
Until in an anointed moment
Becomes joy
I got through
Lots of others have
And so can you.

Postscript 1: Stunned Grief

Mike died today.
My beloved went to sleep
        and didn't wake up.
My lover, my husband, my kindred spirit:
      is gone.

Tears flow and my heart hurts.
The last time we spoke,
he had a ferocious coughing event;
I phoned this morning from Dallas
and no response;
I figured he was in the bathroom.
I phoned again and thought he was
on his way to dialysis.
When he wasn't there,
I knew something was incredibly wrong.
He slipped away
Oh God, my baby,
my sweet, sweet prince is gone;
I can only hear his voice
 on the answering machine.

He was such a marvelous person,
even with the insanity around spending;
God, I need your help.
I need you
to let me know what to do next.

I know this too will pass;
I know my heart will heal;
At this moment, I am incredulous.
He was bigger than life;
he filled up huge spaces;
he was there for me, no matter what.

How does this loss affect who I am?
How does this loss affect
how I relate to his biological family?
How does this shape
    what I do for holidays, everyday?
For the last 28+ years,
lots of my life
    has been around Mike,
    and his thoughts
    and his desires and his needs.
How do I do life now?
What does it mean to be widow?

I must take life one moment at a time:
        stay right with God
        Do the next right thing;
        Trust God for the results;
        Laugh a lot;
        Hit the reset button;
I am grateful he didn't suffer any more.

Post script 2: Baptized Rage, Smoldering Grief

Rage and grief sleep together
as partners within the vicissitudes of my being,
from the numbness of yesterday bursts
raw, visceral emotion weighing heavily on my heart,
almost smothering my spirit,
like the multiple layers of paint
   forged onto vehicles
     made ready for purchase.

What gets me through: faith, family, friends --
In my very bone marrow
   rests an unfaltering faith
   fused by parents and family
   an indefatigable belief, unconditional!

Not meaning that I do not question, even challenge God:
at issue: God is, God cares, God created faith,
Faith in the love we shared for almost three decades:
a vital, spiritual, sensual, intellectual, sexual, physical Love
With parameters as deep as the ocean
as inspiring as majestic sunrises
as fiery and passionate as the "1812 Overture"
and "The Hallelujah Chorus" from *Messiah*.

And when such a relationship changes
Through death – for he is gone in one dimension
   yet very present in others --
the love of God,
  family, and friends
   are those which sustain us.

Post Script 3: Bon Voyage

At the break of dawn
When the sun has not yet
burst open in our midst,
Tears flow, body wracked with pain
The cavernous aching hole
Left by your physical/sensual departure
Widens, deepens
Numb hurt bubbles up.

Experiencing such emotions fully
Allows a release, a letting go
that passes in moments
and peace comes
and memories sing
and moving forward in those moments
Doing the next right thing
Vibrancy embraces me
And I know you are OK.
   And you tried to signal us
   as the beeping
signaling the refrigerator filter
kept going off, relentlessly, not to be quieted
a few days after your departure.

No one loved water,
   Iced water like you.
Thanks for caring enough
to remind me that you
will always be in my
heart, mind, body, soul.
Thank you for having had
   such a bold, audacious spirit
That you dared to invite
   me into your life --
   because you listened for God
and God joined us together;
and you embraced me, loved me,
held me, bragged about me
Unconditionally, relentlessly, lovingly.

And so realizing
the many gifts we shared
Understanding you had been
given five years of borrowed time,
which was actually life support,
   not treatment--
Recognizing you knew the
inevitability of an impending demise –

I will always hold you near and dear.
I release you to be with God,
to know joy unspeakable.

www.ingramcontent.com/pod-product-compliance
Lightning Source LLC
Chambersburg PA
CBHW060604230426
43670CB00011B/1967